The Five-Fold Offices

Embrace Your Gifts To Live A Purpose-Filled Life

Emmanuel Adewusi

CCCG Publishing House

Scriptures are taken from the New King James Version. Copyright 1979, 1980, 1982 by Thomas Nelson, Inc. Used by permission. All right reserved.

Author: Emmanuel Adewusi

ISBN: 978-1-989099-40-7 (hardcover)

ISBN: 978-1-989099-41-4 (ebook)

First Printing 2025

Contents

Dedication

To the apostles, prophets, evangelists, pastors, and teachers who have shaped and influenced my ministry. Your dedication to God's work and commitment to spreading the Gospel have provided invaluable lessons and examples to follow.

Preface

Growing up in the church, I often heard teachings that suggested the Five-Fold Offices mentioned in Ephesians 4 were reserved for those with a specific calling from God. This notion led me to believe that not everyone was part of the Five-Fold Ministry. However, my perspective shifted dramatically one day when I delved into Ephesians 4 and was struck by a profound revelation. This insight marked the beginning of my journey toward understanding how God has equipped all His children for service, regardless of whether they are in full-time ministry or not.

Let's examine Ephesians 4:1-16 and explore the implications of the highlighted words together:

*"I, therefore, the prisoner of the Lord, beseech you to walk worthy of the calling with which you were called, with all lowliness and gentleness, with longsuffering, bearing with one another in love, endeavoring to keep the unity of the Spirit in the bond of peace. There is one body and one Spirit, just as you were called in one hope of your calling; one Lord, one faith, one baptism; one God and Father of all, who is above all, and through all, and in you all. But to **each one of us** grace was given according to the measure of Christ's gift. Therefore He says: 'When He ascended on high, He led captivity captive, and gave gifts **to men.**' (Now this, 'He ascended'—what does it mean but that He also first descended into the lower parts of the earth? He who descended*

is also the One who ascended far above all the heavens, that He might fill all things.) And He Himself gave **some** *to be apostles,* **some** *prophets,* **some** *evangelists, and* **some** *pastors* **and** *teachers, for the equipping of the saints for the work of ministry, for the edifying of the body of Christ, till we* **all** *come to the unity of the faith and of the knowledge of the Son of God, to a perfect man, to the measure of the stature of the fullness of Christ; that we should no longer be children, tossed to and fro and carried about with every wind of doctrine, by the trickery of men, in the cunning craftiness of deceitful plotting, but, speaking the truth in love, may grow up in all things into Him who is the head—Christ—from whom the whole body, joined and knit together by what every joint supplies, according to the effective working by which every part does its share, causes growth of the body for the edifying of itself in love."*

The highlighted words in the passage reveal that Jesus did not reserve these gifts only those in the church with the Five-Fold Offices. We are told that Jesus gave gifts to men. The phrases **"each one"** and **"to men"** suggest that Apostle Paul was addressing all people indicating that every human being has been endowed with these gifts. The second implication is that each person is either an apostle, prophet, evangelist, pastor, or teacher. This conclusion comes from the use of **"some"** when referring to each of the offices. Even if you don't believe that, at the very least, you must recognize that the essence of the Five-Fold Ministry (apostle, pastor, teacher, evangelist, and prophet) is to equip and guide individuals toward growth and understanding. So, either you believe you have already been given the gift, or you believe that the Lord has raised those who will train you into the gift. Therefore, you are either created as an apostle, pastor, prophet, teacher, or evangelist, or you will be nurtured into one of these offices to by others.

To truly grasp the concept of the Five-Fold Ministry and our individual roles within it, we must view it through the lens of God's grand design for humanity. Without this perspective, it becomes challenging to accept our specific roles, no matter how minor they may seem. For instance, without understanding the collective purpose of the body, we might question, "Why am I merely the nail that is constantly being trimmed and polished to look beautiful? Why am I not the heart or the eyes of the body?" Such questions stem from a lack of awareness of God's comprehensive plan for the body. God determines our roles and where we fit into His overarching plan for humanity. Our primary focus as God's children should be to understand our place within the body and enhance our contributions to it.

The discussion on the five offices is crucial because it provides scriptural clarity on identifying our unique identities within the context of God's family. This identity assures us that victory should be a norm in our lives because God's word says that our faith grants us victory over the world (1 John 5:4-5). Anchoring our faith in God, ourselves, and others is critical for successfully dominating in our world. We must trust that God is always good, even when we do not understand His actions or inactions. even when His actions or inactions are beyond our understanding. We must believe that God knew what He was doing when He created us with our unique gifts. Additionally, we must trust that God intentionally surrounds us with people whose gifts complement ours.

I pray that this book serves as a guiding light on your journey to understanding and fulfilling your role within the Five-Fold Ministry. May it inspire, challenge, and equip you to walk boldly in God's purpose.

1

Overview of the Five-Fold Offices

The framework of the Five-Fold Offices is rooted in Scripture:

"And He Himself gave some to be apostles, some prophets, some evangelists, and some pastors and teachers, for the equipping of the saints for the work of ministry, for the edifying of the body of Christ, till we all come to the unity of the faith and of the knowledge of the Son of God, to a perfect man, to the measure of the stature of the fullness of Christ." (Ephesians 4:11-13)

These offices each carry unique, God-given functions. While each serves a specific purpose, they are interdependent, working in harmony to serve others and bring balance to ministries, teams, and organizations. When these offices operate in unity, they provide a full expression of Christ's grace and power, extending their impact beyond the Church into societal spheres such as corporate leadership, education, healthcare, and community service. Understanding the grace at work in each office not only transforms the group but also the individual, shaping us into the image of Christ as we grow in our calling.

MY PERSONAL JOURNEY

I can vividly recall my own journey, beginning as a prophet and gradually growing into the apostolic, pastoral, teaching, and eventually the evangelistic graces. Of all the offices, the evangelistic was the hardest for me to connect with. My upbringing, personality, worldview, and limited understanding of the evangelistic office made it difficult. However, as I grew in knowledge, maturity, and love, I recognized the beauty and necessity of the evangelistic grace, especially as I sought to grow the ministries I lead—CCCG (Cornerstone Christian Church of God) and HoM (Hour of Meditation)—where the apostolic grace is strong.

While these ministries have strong systems and leaders who align with the vision, the calling to reach the nations demands the evangelistic grace. I began to desire this grace deeply and took intentional steps to align myself with it. I sought out strong evangelists, honoured their gifts, and learned from their approach. Over time, I began to see myself functioning more effectively as an evangelist, particularly as the ministry expanded into new territories.

In the early days of this ministry, I remember being struck by how differently the evangelists responded during our services. While most people sat quietly, taking in the Word as I preached, the evangelists were a burst of energy. They couldn't contain themselves—they'd cheer me on with such passion that it felt like they were preaching with me! At first, I must admit, it caught me off guard. Even the apostles in the ministry would glance their way, some with curiosity, others with raised eyebrows.

But as I reflected on it, I began to see their response in a new light. Their enthusiasm wasn't a disruption; it was a powerful contribution. They were bringing life and energy to the room, fuelling the atmosphere in a way only they could. It reminded me that every office carries its own distinct expression—its quirks, strengths, and even its challenges. But when these offices come together, they create a divine harmony, completing the body of Christ as God intended.

As a leader, I've made it a priority to ensure that every office has a place to thrive within the ministry. At CCCG, we intentionally create platforms for each office to flourish. For example, pastors lead our community group, while evangelists drive outreach events in the community. This ensures that the vision remains balanced and all graces are fully expressed. Without intentionality, it's easy for a ministry or organization to reflect only the dominant traits of its leader, but that's not what we're called to do. We're not meant to raise people to be like us; we're meant to help them become the best version of themselves, growing into the fullness of their unique calling.

For some, this book will help you discover yourself and love your office. For others, it will elevate your understanding of people and expand your heart to accept and honour the offices of others. And for those who already understand and embrace the Five-Fold Offices as God intended, my prayer is that you will go even further—embracing the grace at work in other offices so that you can operate like Jesus, who embodied all five.

As you read, consider: What office do you naturally resonate with? Which office do you struggle to relate with? These questions can help you uncover where God has called you to begin your journey. Embrace the process, and let God shape you into the fullness of His calling for your life.

THE FIVE-FOLD OFFICES

Apostles

Apostles are considered pioneers or 'sent ones' with a unique calling to establish and build new churches, ministries, or movements. They provide foundational leadership and governance to align churches and other institutions with their mission and vision. Beyond the church environment, apostles are often visionaries and strategists in corporate settings, driving innovation and establishing new initiatives. They are natural leaders who excel in solving complex problems and sustaining new ventures, ensuring that organizations have a solid foundation and clear direction. In business, apostles are akin to entrepreneurial leaders who identify opportunities, create new business ventures, and set long-term strategic goals.

Modern Day Examples: Bill Gates and Mark Zukerberg.

Prophets

Prophets convey divine or strategic messages to people, with the capacity to see visions and dreams. They deliver insights and revelations that guide institutions and individuals alike. Prophets are essential in guiding the church and societal structures by providing direction and promoting alignment with core values and missions. In professional contexts, prophets are akin to analysts and consultants who interpret data and trends to provide strategic insights. Their role involves projecting future trends, offering innovative solutions, and ensuring that organizations remain aligned with their mission and values.

Modern Day Examples: Martin Luther King Jr. and Steve Jobs.

Evangelists

Evangelists possess a unique gift for spreading messages far and wide with passion and energy that stirs people's hearts. They are highly effective communicators who engage believers and non-believers, influencing various spheres of society, including media, education, and social justice initiatives. In corporate settings, evangelists function as enthusiastic brand ambassadors and communicators, spreading the company's message and building relationships with new customers and stakeholders. Their ability to engage, inspire, and motivate others makes them invaluable in marketing, public relations, and customer engagement roles.

Modern Day Examples: Donald Trump and Oprah Winfrey.

Pastors

Pastors, also known as shepherds, have a nurturing and caregiving role within the church and beyond. They ensure the well-being of their congregations and communities by providing spiritual nourishment, counselling, and guidance in various settings, such as counselling centers, hospitals, and community organizations. In professional environments, pastors serve as essential caregivers and managers who ensure the well-being and care of clients and employees. Their empathetic nature fosters a nurturing environment where individuals can thrive. Pastors provide emotional support, conflict resolution, and holistic care in sectors like healthcare, education, and social work.

Modern Day Examples: Simon Sinek and Mary Teresa Bojaxhiu MC (a.k.a Mother Teresa).

Teachers

Teachers impart knowledge and understanding, breaking down complex principles into digestible and applicable lessons. Their role is crucial in grounding individuals in foundational truths and equipping them with practical skills. Beyond the church, teachers provide educational insights in academic and professional environments. They are responsible for instructing in sound principles and making complex concepts accessible and understandable. Teachers collaborate with subject matter experts and instructional designers in academic and corporate training settings to create engaging and compelling learning experiences. Their role ensures the preservation, accurate conveyance, and correct interpretation of knowledge, fostering a culture of continuous learning and development.

Modern Day Examples: Michelle Obama and Seth Godin.

CONVERSATIONS ABOUT IDENTITY

"Then the word of the Lord came to me, saying, 'Before I formed you in the womb, I knew you; before you were born, I sanctified you; I ordained you as a prophet to the nations.'' Then said I: "Ah, Lord God! Behold, I cannot speak, for I am a youth.'" (Jeremiah 1:4-6)

Knowing Your True Identity in God

The journey to discovering your true identity begins with divine revelation of who God says you are. This process is similar to your parents or caregivers sharing the details of your birth and early years—information you wouldn't be able to access without them. Confidence emerges when you grasp the truth about who you are in God's eyes. However, some believers negotiate rather than accept God's defined purpose for them. They might say, "I don't want to be a teacher; I want to be a pastor," or, "I don't want to be an apostle; I want to be a prophet." When God declares you an evangelist, don't argue or offer excuses. He knew you before you were aware of yourself, just as God corrected Jeremiah when he hesitated about his calling.

"But the Lord said to me: 'Do not say, 'I am a youth,' For you shall go to all to whom I send you, And whatever I command you, you shall speak. Do not be afraid of their faces, For I am with you to deliver you,' says the Lord. Then the Lord put forth His hand and touched my mouth, and the Lord said to me: 'Behold, I have put My words in your mouth.'" (Jeremiah 1:7-9)

God's touch on Jeremiah's mouth affirmed his prophetic calling despite his initial self-doubt. Similarly, Moses, despite being described as "mighty in words and deeds" in Egypt (Acts 7:22), later struggled with his speech. But God can endow an evangelist with the energy needed to convey His message or touch a prophet's eyes, heart, and ears to enhance their spiritual perception and hearing:

"Moreover the word of the Lord came to me, saying, 'Jeremiah, what do you see?' And I said, 'I see a branch of an almond tree.' Then the Lord said to me, 'You have seen well, for I am ready to perform My word.' And the word of the Lord came to me the second time, saying, 'What do you see?' And I said, 'I see a boiling pot, and it is facing away from the north.'" (Jeremiah 1:11-13)

Never leave your conversations with God incomplete, as Jeremiah did initially. Some people end their spiritual dialogues prematurely, leaving with confusion rather than clarity. Jeremiah learned to recognize and articulate his visions accurately through his interactions with God, growing from seeing simple objects to discerning more complex prophetic warnings.

This journey from uncertain to confident prophecy highlights the necessity of humility and a teachable spirit.

It's not enough to acknowledge your role, such as being a teacher; you must let God instruct you on how to fulfill it effectively. This includes learning when to speak or remain silent, the appropriate language, and recognizing those who might appear as genuine followers but are wolves in disguise.

Conversations with Parents, Mentors, and Other Authorities

When discovering your identity, it is vital to seek guidance from the right people—those who have observed your growth and have had the privilege of experiencing different stages of your life. Parents, guardians, long-term mentors, and other trusted authorities are often well-positioned to provide valuable insights into your personality and development.

Life's experiences can shape and sometimes distort our personalities in ways we might not even realize. For example, you might have been very expressive as a child but became more passive and inarticulate after facing academic setbacks. Or perhaps you were bold and adventurous in your younger years but grew timid and withdrawn following a traumatic event. Conversations with those who know you well can help uncover these shifts, offering clarity about who you were before life's challenges influenced you.

These conversations are particularly meaningful because, as Scripture says, *"By the mouth of two or three witnesses every word shall be established."* (2 Corinthians 13:1) It's important to recognize, however, that no one person will remember every detail of your life. Instead, they are likely to recall key highlights while forgetting other significant moments. By consulting multiple trusted authorities, you can piece together a fuller and more accurate picture of your personality, traits, and potential.

Approach these conversations with humility and openness, recognizing that they are a tool to help you rediscover and embrace your true, God-ordained identity. At the same time, be mindful that while others may offer their opinions, they must never outweigh what the Lord has declared about you. Let God's Word be the unshakable foundation of your identity and the ultimate authority over who you are.

THRIVE IN YOUR NATURAL GIFTING

Identifying your unique gift and fully committing to it is essential. Life is too short to spend it striving on paths that do not align with your innate strengths. Deciding whether to serve as an apostle, pastor, or another role should be guided by where your God-given talents naturally shine. At first glance, it might seem that only a select few in the church hold notable roles, while the rest support them. However, the Bible reveals that gifts are given to everyone. Recognizing this truth broadens our perspective, showing that many individuals—even those outside the church—possess these talents. Excellent teachers, persuasive marketers (like evangelists), and visionary leaders (apostles) often exhibit these gifts without even realizing their spiritual significance. The key is to identify your gift and start using it to advance God's kingdom and enrich your life.

Reflecting on my journey, I realize that subtle indicators of my prophetic gift were present even in my childhood. I had an unusual ability to sense and predict outcomes—a gift I would later recognize as prophetic. One vivid memory stands out: during power outages in Lagos, Nigeria, I often sat in the dark, feeling an inexplicable assurance about when the electricity would be restored. My siblings looked at me skeptically, yet time and again, my predictions proved accurate. At the time, I didn't fully grasp the significance of this ability. Still, it was the first indication of my prophetic gift—a connection to the spiritual realm that would eventually define my calling.

As I grew older, my understanding of my prophetic calling deepened. I vividly recall a moment when I was reading the Bible and felt a strong prompting from the Holy Spirit to reach out to a friend. I sent a text message containing specific guidance I felt compelled to share. To my surprise, my friend called back almost immediately, expressing that my words were precisely the answer he needed and that he had been asking the Holy Spirit for at that very moment. This and several other experiences solidified my conviction that I am a prophet.

The journey to accept and embrace my prophetic gift wasn't always easy, but it became a foundational part of my personal growth. Initially, I wrestled with many insecurities, but through intentional reflection and the pursuit of healing, I began to see the value of my gifts. Embracing my prophetic gifting has been a deeply transformative experience, shaping my understanding of purpose and the meaningful ways I can influence the lives of others. Today, I confidently use my prophetic gift to serve God and the world around me, unshaken by fear or doubt.

YOU ARE EMPOWERED FOR PURPOSE

When you embrace your unique gifts, God's grace will abound to equip you for your divine purpose. Grace is apportioned to each of us based on the revelation of Christ's gift within us.

Understanding your role within the Five-Fold framework clarifies the *why* of your existence, aligning you with God's grand plan. As Scripture declares, *"To each one of us, grace was given according to the measure of Christ's gift."* (*Ephesians 4:7*) This means God has already equipped you with everything you need to thrive in your calling—it's not something you are waiting to receive. However, many of us are still learning to recognize and fully utilize this grace.

Imagine it as a perfectly tailored gift that's been handed to you. The challenge lies in opening it and understanding its contents. For instance, think of a fish in water: it moves with ease and purpose, completely in its element. But take that same fish out of the water, and it struggles. In the same way, when you align with your divine purpose, you operate with grace and effortlessness. The Holy Spirit is here to help you identify your gifts and use them effectively. You don't need to strive for what you already possess—God has placed His Spirit within you and surrounded you with others who complement your gifts. Once you align yourself with His plan, you'll find the fulfillment, grace, and confidence to thrive in your calling.

As you read through the chapters that follow, let is be your mirror —who do you see? Are you the apostle, prophet, evangelist, pastor, or teacher? **You are empowered for purpose.** Through the revelation of your identity and gifts, God will enable you to live a life of meaning and impact. Let's begin this journey of discovery together.

2

The Apostolic Office

INTRODUCTION TO THE APOSTOLIC OFFICE

The apostolic office is foundational, the first office established after Christ's resurrection. Jesus Himself exemplified the apostolic role, demonstrating its significance by operating in all five offices and laying the groundwork for what would become the Church. In fact, Hebrews 3:1 refers to Him as *"the Apostle and High Priest of our confession."* Apostles are sent ones equipped to establish and strengthen churches, ministries, and movements, while influencing various sectors of society with Kingdom principles.

At its core, the apostolic office is about building foundations. Apostles carry the weight of creating order and structure where none exists. They are entrusted with blueprints that ensure what they establish is enduring. Without their guidance, the efforts of other offices may lack the cohesion needed for long-term impact. Imagine constructing a building and attempting to pour the foundation last; such an approach would lead to collapse. Similarly, apostles are the first to arrive on the scene to lay the groundwork upon which others can build.

Apostles are catalysts for growth and innovation, venturing into uncharted territory to bring God's purposes to fruition. Whether they are starting a new church, launching a ministry, or introducing Kingdom principles into businesses or education systems, apostles lead with vision, clarity, and a deep sense of purpose.

The Apostolic Calling

The apostolic office holds a unique sequence and significance within the Five-Fold Ministry. 1 Corinthians 12:28, *"And God has appointed these in the church: first apostles, second prophets, third teachers..."* This order reflects the foundational role apostles play. Their placement as first among the offices is not a matter of superiority but of sequence—they determine what goes where and establish the steps to take.

While every office carries leadership qualities, apostles are graced to provide the initial framework upon which the other offices—prophets, teachers, pastors, and evangelists—can thrive. They set the vision and create the blueprint for building, ensuring alignment with God's purpose.

As Ephesians 2:20 states, *"Having been built on the foundation of the apostles and prophets, Jesus Christ Himself being the chief cornerstone,"* the Church's foundation rests upon the work of apostles and prophets, with Christ as the cornerstone holding everything together. This underscores the significance of the apostolic role as not only foundational but also integrative, ensuring that all aspects of the Kingdom—spiritual, relational, and practical—are aligned.

It is important to emphasize that no one office is superior to another. Each plays a vital role in the Body of Christ, much like different organs in the human body. However, the apostolic office leads the sequence, much like the foundation of a building precedes its walls, roof, or windows. Each part is essential, but the foundation sets the stage for everything else to function effectively.

CHARACTERISTICS OF AN APOSTLE

Leader

Leadership is a grace that comes naturally to apostles, marked by their ability to inspire, direct, and mobilize others toward a shared goal. This capacity for leadership extends beyond vision or strategy; it is rooted in an innate ability to unite people, build trust, and foster alignment among diverse individuals or groups. As an apostle, you are called to lead with authority and purpose that encourages others to follow, even in uncertain or challenging situations.

Leading through complexity is one of the marks of this calling. Your confidence and calm presence in the face of challenges reassure those you lead, instilling trust and a shared sense of determination. As an apostle, you understand that effective leadership isn't about control but about influence—guiding others toward outcomes that serve the greater purpose.

For many apostles, these traits would have been evident from a young age. You might have been called "bossy" or "controlling" because of their natural inclination to step up and take charge. Qualities like decisiveness, focus, and a sharp sense of responsibility might have been misunderstood as being heartless, detached, or even ruthless. However, these qualities are the early indicators of your ability to lead and establish order in which sphere you are called to.

Visionary

Apostles are visionaries, divinely gifted to see the big picture and chart a path forward with clarity and purpose. Their foresight allows them to discern future needs and opportunities, positioning organizations and ministries for sustainable growth and lasting impact. Apostles excel at bringing alignment to people and organizations, ensuring everyone remains focused on the problem they have come together to solve. Apostles clarify the mission, stripping away distractions and uniting teams around a common purpose. This focus keeps efforts intentional and impactful, ensuring that every step taken moves the vision closer to fulfillment.

As an apostle, you don't just see the future, you have a passion and gift to lead others into it. You have the charisma to present ideals to people that you need to get to the destination you have envisioned. You will find that you are not satisfied with temporary wins; you build with the future in mind, ensuring the foundation is strong enough to sustain what God desires to accomplish. Everything you do is with purpose in mind. You always have to loop it every decision as a leader to the "why". Your leadership anchors organizations in purpose, driving them toward growth, transformation, and Kingdom advancement.

Process Thinker

Apostles don't just dream big; they are architects of the future, designing actionable plans that align with long-term goals. They possess a unique ability to break down large tasks into smaller, manageable steps, making progress toward a greater vision achievable. This strategic mindset enables them to navigate complexity with clarity and purpose.

Their ability to process and plan is invaluable in project management, organizational development, and ministry planning. Apostles excel at taking complex problems and crafting step-by-step solutions that drive initiatives forward. By understanding both the end goal and the path to get there, they ensure that projects are executed efficiently and effectively.

This gift of thinking in processes empowers apostles to lead with intentionality, transforming lofty ideas into actionable strategies. This is why people are willing to follow them. Apostles don't just reveal the vision—they clearly outline the steps to achieve it. Their skill in balancing the big picture with the finer details makes them highly effective in bringing visions to life and inspiring others to follow the plan with confidence.

Problem Solver

Apostles are naturally drawn to challenges—whether they involve people, systems, or processes. Problems gravitate toward them because of their capacity to address them effectively. Life without problems to solve can feel uninspiring to an apostle. The presence of challenges energizes them, offering opportunities to innovate, build, and contribute to meaningful change.

A key aspect of their problem-solving ability lies in their prophetic insight, which enables them to perceive patterns, connect dots, and derive strategic direction. This goes beyond conventional problem-solving by tapping into inspiration through visions, dreams, or words of knowledge.

Prophetic insight is the ability to draw inspiration for solutions that others might overlook. Apostles can discern connections between seemingly unrelated elements, bringing clarity and direction where complexity or confusion may exist. This insight allows them to devise strategies that address not only surface-level issues but also root causes, ensuring sustainable outcomes.

Entrepreneurial Spirit

Apostles are natural entrepreneurs, gifted to start and build initiatives with clarity, vision, and purpose. They excel in creating structure, organizing steps, and ensuring effective execution. Their entrepreneurial ability goes beyond inventing new ideas; it often involves innovating within existing frameworks or expanding on established concepts.

As an apostle, you always have an idea to start something new or do something different or in a better way. You are driven by a desire to create meaningful impact, apostles explore new opportunities across ministry, business, education, and social enterprise. As visionaries, they see potential where others may not and mobilize resources to bring those ideas to life. They are trailblazers, setting the standard for excellence and innovation while paving the way for others to follow.

In the early stages of launching an idea, apostles demonstrate adaptability and resilience by wearing many hats. Your leadership grace allows you to draw from the strengths of other offices to meet the immediate needs of the vision. However, your ability to identify, attract, and empower others is critical to the long-term success of any project. By delegating tasks to capable burden bearers, you will be able to focus on where you thrive the most – in strategic oversight – without being bogged down by day-to-day operations.

Versatile

Apostles embody a rare combination of adaptability and insight, enabling them to thrive in any situation and turn challenges into opportunities for growth. They carry a broad knowledge base, knowing just enough about various areas to connect the dots and bring different elements together effectively. This breadth of understanding enables them to address complex challenges with a holistic perspective, fostering innovation and uncovering solutions that others may overlook.

This versatility makes apostles adaptable in any environment, whether they are leading in the church, navigating corporate structures, or driving community transformation. They have the God-given ability to bridge gaps, unite teams, and align efforts toward a shared vision. By integrating diverse elements seamlessly, apostles create systems and structures that not only achieve goals but elevate everyone involved.

Their combination of flexibility and insight reflects a heart attuned to the Holy Spirit, allowing them to discern the best course of action in ever-changing circumstances. This gift positions apostles as dynamic leaders who inspire others to embrace adaptability and see challenges as opportunities to demonstrate God's wisdom and excellence.

Receive New Revelation

Apostles are uniquely equipped to receive fresh revelation, injecting new insights that transform the body of Christ and inspire growth. These revelations serve as a foundation for progress, as teachers expand on them to bring deeper understanding and practical application. Beyond the church, apostles carry this same grace into areas like business, education, and governance, bringing ideas that challenge conventional thinking and spark transformation.

This ability to receive and implement new revelation mirrors the disruptive innovations we see in other fields. Consider the rise of artificial intelligence (AI), a technology that has revolutionized industries by introducing groundbreaking ways to solve problems, analyze data, and improve efficiency. Generative AI, for example, can produce creative solutions to complex challenges, opening doors to opportunities that once seemed impossible. Similarly, apostles are called to introduce divine strategies and frameworks that shift paradigms and open new possibilities, whether in ministry or the marketplace.

As Scripture declares, *"Which in other ages was not made known to the sons of men, as it has now been revealed by the Spirit to His holy apostles and prophets."* (Ephesians 3:5) Apostles carry this mantle of revelation, breaking barriers and paving the way for the Church and the world to walk in unprecedented wisdom and innovation.

Dogged Determination and Perseverance

"Truly the signs of an apostle were accomplished among you with all perseverance, in signs and wonders and mighty deeds." (2 Corinthians 12:12)

Apostles are marked by an unrelenting resilience that reflects their divine assignment. Like a foundation that remains standing even after everything built upon it has crumbled, they possess an inner strength fueled by their unwavering trust in God. Apostles are not merely visionaries; they are finishers—driven to start what God has placed in their hearts, labor tirelessly to see it succeed, and sustain it until it is ready to be entrusted to others for further building.

Their perseverance is not circumstantial but rooted in their calling. Apostles remain steadfast in the face of trials, knowing that challenges are part of the process. They understand that what they build is meant to last long after their part is done. This dogged determination is a defining characteristic of apostles. It ensures that the work they do is not only effective and impactful but eternal, laying a foundation that others can build upon and advancing the Kingdom in ways that only perseverance can achieve.

Can Function Without Encouragement

Apostles possess a remarkable ability to stay motivated from within, driven by the vision God has entrusted to them. This intrinsic motivation does not depend on applause, recognition, or external validation. Instead, it flows from a deep understanding of their calling and a conviction to see the work through, no matter the challenges they face.

As Paul writes, *"Nor did we seek glory from men, either from you or from others, when we might have made demands as apostles of Christ."* (1 Thessalonians 2:6) Apostles embody this same spirit, refusing to rely on human praise or approval to fuel their mission. Their drive comes from knowing they are fulfilling a divine purpose, which is far greater than the opinions or affirmations of others.

Whether planting a church, launching a new initiative, or leading a transformative project, apostles remain focused and resolute, drawing strength from their connection with God. Their capacity to function without encouragement enables them to remain steadfast, even when the journey is lonely or difficult.

Identify Gifts in Others

Apostles carry a remarkable ability to discern and recognize the gifts in others, much like Jesus identified the potential in Peter and Andrew, calling them to become fishers of men. *"Follow Me, and I will make you fishers of men."* (Matthew 4:19) This divine insight allows apostles to see people not just as they are, but as who they could become, and to guide them into fulfilling their God-ordained potential.

This gift is essential for developing leadership teams and empowering individuals in various spheres of life. Apostles often take on mentorship roles to help and guide others to uncover their unique gifts and callings while positioning them in roles where they can thrive and contribute effectively. True mentorship, however, is not about molding someone into a replica of the mentor or forcing them into a preconceived mold. Instead, it's about nurturing the mentee into the person God created them to be. Through mentorship, they replicate the greatness God has unlocked in them, ensuring their legacy extends far beyond their own work.

GROWTH AREAS FOR APOSTLES

Patience

Apostles, with their strong visionary nature, often struggle with patience when others do not progress as quickly toward objectives. Their sense of urgency can lead to frustration, as they are ready to run the moment they see a vision. This impatience may strain relationships, leading apostles to say things like, *"I have been repeating the same thing to you repeatedly. I'm done with you, you are wasting my time, you do not want to learn."*

However, patience is vital for apostles to effectively lead and nurture those they are called to guide. They must recognize that not everyone moves at the same pace or processes things the same way. The wisdom in Habakkuk 2:3 offers valuable perspective: *"For the vision is yet for an appointed time; But at the end it will speak, and it will not lie. Though it tarries, wait for it; Because it will surely come, it will not tarry."*

A key to developing patience lies in understanding God's timing. You must intentionally seek discernment through prayer, asking God to reveal His times and seasons. Ecclesiastes 3 reminds us that everything has its time. When God shows you a vision, it is crucial to understand whether it pertains to the past, present, or future. Just because a vision is revealed now does not mean it is meant to manifest immediately. It may take years to come to fruition. Misinterpreting the timing can lead to frustration, burnout for the people they lead, and assignments given prematurely to those not yet ready to handle them.

While you can see the potential in others, you must also be mindful of their current capacity and capabilities. Driving people too hard or too fast can be damaging, even when the goal is good. An apostle's leadership ensures people reach their destination, but the state in which they arrive matters just as much as the destination itself. By balancing vision with patience, you can inspire growth and achieve results without overwhelming those they are called to lead.

Managing Pride

Leadership, with its achievements and accolades, can easily become a breeding ground for pride. For apostles, the challenge is heightened by the abundance of revelation they receive—revelation that can be awe-inspiring and transformative. This grace to see the end from the beginning, coupled with successful leadership results, can unintentionally lead to arrogance or a sense of superiority. Apostles may begin to look down on others, becoming demeaning or dismissive of those who do not share their level of insight or understanding.

To guard against pride, apostles must cultivate humility intentionally. Leadership is not just about achieving results; it is about balancing tasks and goals with the safety, security, and dignity of the people they are leading. It is crucial to remember that leadership is service, not status. Asking God to fill your heart with love for people ensures that your focus remains on building others up, not just driving toward outcomes.

Accountability is a vital tool in managing pride. As an apostle, you should surround yourself with trusted individuals who can speak the truth in love, offering correction when needed and helping you stay grounded. These accountability partners are critical in ensuring that success does not lead to detachment or arrogance but instead fuels greater collaboration and service.

Additionally, allow others to assist you, even when you know you can complete tasks on your own. This not only fosters teamwork but also prevents the subtle pride that comes from feeling self-sufficient. Leadership is most impactful when it is shared, creating an environment where everyone contributes to the vision.

Task-Oriented Communication

Apostles, driven by their focus on achieving goals, may unintentionally prioritize tasks over relationships. This task-oriented approach, while effective for progress, can sometimes overlook the importance of personal connections and emotional intelligence. Without relational awareness, team cohesion may suffer, leading to reduced morale and diminished collaboration.

This challenge often extends beyond professional settings and into personal relationships. You may find that you are so consumed by the vision you are running with that you unintentionally neglect the emotional needs of your loved ones. Balancing work with personal connections requires apostles to be intentional about creating time and space to nurture relationships outside of their mission. Maintaining strong and meaningful connections with your family and friends will provide a foundation of support and refreshment that sustains you in your calling.

Leading with Love

Apostles are called to balance their visionary pursuits with a deep and genuine care for the well-being of those they lead. While your drive to achieve goals is vital, it must be tempered with sensitivity and compassion to ensure your leadership does not become overbearing or insensitive. True apostolic leadership is marked not only by progress but also by the trust and support cultivated along the way.

Understanding the stories and situations of the people you lead stirs up compassion, enabling apostles to connect on a deeper level. This awareness fosters empathy and strengthens relationships, ensuring that those under their leadership feel valued and understood. By taking the time to listen and learn about individual experiences, apostles can lead with greater wisdom and grace.

Avoiding Isolation

As an apostle, you may find that you tend to isolate yourself from others—particularly when you are working with people who are still figuring things out. Your ability to understand the full scope of tasks and execute them independently can make collaboration feel inefficient or frustrating. This frustration is often amplified when you encounter people who require constant encouragement or reassurance, which may clash with your task-oriented mindset.

However, isolation can limit both impact and growth. As the saying goes, *"You can go fast by going alone, but you cannot go far by yourself."* Apostles must learn to pause, even when you know the steps ahead, and wait for others to catch up. This patience fosters team unity and ensures shared success.

To overcome isolation, prioritize building meaningful relationships and seek regular input and collaboration from others. Reading resources like *How to Win Friends and Influence People* by Dale Carnegie or *Becoming a People Person* by John Maxwell can provide practical strategies for improving interpersonal connections. Engaging with peers and mentors not only prevents burnout but also offers a broader perspective and new insights that enhances your leadership.

Receiving Appreciation

Apostles often focus so intensely on their mission that they overlook or dismiss appreciation from others. You might view recognition as unnecessary or even a distraction, believing that your work speaks for itself.

To grow in this area, reframe how they view appreciation—not as a detour, but as an essential form of encouragement and connection. Accepting recognition allows others to contribute to your journey and fosters mutual respect and trust. Celebrating milestones, no matter how small, creates opportunities for gratitude and strengthens relationships with those you lead.

Overcoming Imposter Syndrome

Young apostles often grapple with imposter syndrome, questioning qualifications or authority—especially when you are tasked with leading individuals who are older or more experienced. This internal struggle can sow seeds of self-doubt, making it challenging to lead with the confidence their calling requires. When Jeremiah doubted his ability to lead, God reassured him: *"Do not say, 'I am too young.'"* (Jeremiah 1:7) This reminder emphasizes the importance of placing your confidence in God's grace rather than personal ability, even in the face of criticism or uncertainty.

To combat imposter syndrome, young apostles must surround themselves with a strong support system of mentors and sponsors. These trusted voices provide not only reassurance but also valuable guidance and constructive feedback, helping to anchor you when self-doubt arises. Mentors are there to affirm your divine calling and offer a broader perspective, enabling you to focus on God's purpose rather than your perceived shortcomings.

BIBLICAL EXAMPLES OF APOSTLES

Apostle Paul

Paul demonstrated characteristic perseverance, leadership, and the reception of new revelations. His missionary journeys and epistles offered essential doctrines for the church's formation. *"Paul, a bondservant of Christ Jesus, called to be an apostle and separated to the gospel of God."* (Romans 1:1) His influence extended beyond the church, impacting various communities and cultures. Paul's ability to adapt to different cultures and contexts made him a highly effective apostle whose teachings continue to influence Christian thought and practice.

Apostle Peter

Peter was a natural leader who played a critical role in the early church, including preaching at Pentecost and guiding the church through crucial formative years. *"And I also say to you that you are Peter, and on this rock I will build My church, and the gates of Hades shall not prevail against it."* (Matthew 16:18) Peter's leadership and boldness were instrumental in establishing the early church. His letters provide valuable guidance for church leadership and Christian living.

Deborah

Deborah led Israel through crucial periods, providing both spiritual and political guidance. *"Now Deborah, a prophetess, the wife of Lapidoth, was judging Israel at that time."* (Judges 4:4) Her leadership extended to national matters, showcasing the wide-ranging influence of the apostolic office. Deborah's wisdom and courage were pivotal in delivering Israel from oppression and securing peace.

Joshua

Joshua stepped into Moses' shoes, leading the Israelites into the Promised Land and ensuring God's promises were fulfilled. *"Behold, this day I am going the way of all the earth, and you know in all your hearts and in all your souls that not one thing has failed of all the good things which the Lord your God spoke concerning you. All have come to pass for you; not one word of them has failed."* (Joshua 23:14) Joshua's military and spiritual leadership were crucial in establishing Israel in the Promised Land, demonstrating the importance of faithfulness and obedience to God's commands.

Esther

Esther exemplified apostolic leadership by strategizing to save her people, demonstrating courage and strategic planning. *"Yet who knows whether you have come to the kingdom for such a time as this?"* (Esther 4:14) Her influence in a secular royal court highlights the broader applicability of the apostolic office. Esther's bravery and wisdom were instrumental in preventing the genocide of her people and securing their safety.

3

The Prophetic Office

INTRODUCTION TO THE PROPHETIC OFFICE

The prophetic office is a sacred and weighty calling, distinct from the occasional operation of the gift of prophecy. Prophets are God's watchmen, strategically positioned to guide, protect, and align His people with His divine will. Prophets are responsible for communicating life, direction, and correction that leads the body of Christ toward fulfilling her destiny.

Unlike the gift of prophecy, which can flow temporarily through any believer, the prophetic office is a lifelong mandate marked by a unique grace and a cluster of spiritual gifts. Prophets do not merely deliver messages; they create pathways for God's will to manifest on earth. They possess the authority to dismantle what opposes His kingdom, establish what reflects His glory, and reshape destinies through their words. As Jeremiah 1:10 declares: *"See, I have this day set you over the nations and over the kingdoms, to root out and to pull down, to destroy and to throw down, to build and to plant."*

The prophetic calling demands humility, intimacy with God, and unwavering obedience. A prophet cannot afford to be driven by ambition or personal agendas; their assignment is to steward God's voice with precision and integrity. Walking in this office is not about recognition but a deep partnership with the Creator to ensure His plans happen.

Testing the Prophetic Word

The prophetic office carries immense authority, and with that authority comes the need for accountability. Every prophetic word must be tested—not by emotions or appearances but by the unchanging standard of God's Word. True prophecy will never contradict Scripture, misrepresent God's character, or lead His people astray.

Deuteronomy 13:1-3 provides a framework for discernment:

"If there arises among you a prophet or a dreamer of dreams, and he gives you a sign or a wonder, and the sign or the wonder comes to pass, of which he spoke to you, saying, 'Let us go after other gods'—which you have not known—'and let us serve them,' you shall not listen to the words of that prophet or that dreamer of dreams, for the Lord your God is testing you to know whether you love the Lord your God with all your heart and with all your soul."

A prophetic word may appear accurate, but its source must align with God's truth. True prophecy should never sow fear or confusion. It strengthens, clarifies, and inspires deeper intimacy with God. Authentic prophecy builds faith and points people to Christ. Like Pharaoh's magicians who mimicked Moses, false prophets operate in counterfeit power, seeking to manipulate and mislead.

Prophets are not called to elevate themselves but to glorify God and lead His people closer to Him. Their role is to ensure the church remains sensitive to God's leading, steadfast in truth, and unshaken by the counterfeit. Prophets must walk in humility and reverence, knowing their words carry eternal consequences. Authentic prophets are not motivated by personal gain or recognition. Their messages flow from deep intimacy with God, reflecting His love, wisdom, and holiness.

CHARACTERISTICS OF A PROPHET

Strong Gift of Intuition, Visualization, and Imagination

Prophets are uniquely equipped with extraordinary intuition, visualization, and imagination—abilities often evident even in childhood. What may have seemed like playful imagination was often an early sign of prophetic grace, designed to connect deeply with the supernatural realm.

Prophets operate through three primary channels of divine connection:

- **Seers (Seeing Prophets):** They receive vivid, supernatural visions that unveil God's plans, strategies, or warnings. These visual insights bring clarity and guidance to His people, bridging the gap between heaven and earth.

- **Perceiving Prophets:** Their heightened intuition allows them to sense God's heart, discern spiritual realities, and perceive hidden truths. This grace requires careful alignment with the Holy Spirit to interpret and deliver messages accurately.

- **Hearing Prophets:** Their gift lies in hearing the voice of God with precision, whether through internal impressions or audible direction. These divine words often carry specific instructions and timely insights for the church.

These are sacred gifts designed to reveal God's will and edify His people. However, they must be anchored in the Word of God to avoid misinterpretation or misuse. Spend time in His presence, submit your revelations to trusted spiritual leaders, and cultivate your gift under the guidance of the Holy Spirit.

Extreme Emotional Life

Prophets often experience extreme emotions. This is not a flaw but a foundational characteristic of their calling. We see this vividly in the lives of Elijah and Jeremiah—men who felt deeply, expressed boldly, and carried the burden of their words with intensity. Prophets are custodians of words, and words are not just sounds or letters; they are spirits, and spirits carry emotions. This is why their words are so impactful. They come alive, resonating with the depth of the emotions that birthed them.

The connection between emotions and words is undeniable. When people feel deeply—whether joy, sympathy, or sorrow—they naturally speak out. It is the same for prophets, but on an amplified scale. Their heightened emotional capacity allows them to produce words that are not only timely but also infused with power, authority, and longevity. Their emotions, both extreme and intense, often determine the weight and lasting impact of the words they deliver.

This emotional sensitivity is what enables prophets to connect with the heart of God and the needs of His people. It allows them to feel what others feel, hear what others cannot hear, and speak with a depth that pierces the soul. It is part of what makes the prophetic so unique and so vital to the body of Christ.

Emotional Sensitivity and Obedience

Prophets are often surprised by their emotional responses to God's messages. They don't just hear God's words—they feel His heart. Whether it's His joy, grief, or righteous anger, these emotions can weigh heavily. This heightened emotional connection is both a gift and a responsibility. It allows you to deliver God's messages with authenticity and compassion, ensuring that His heart is felt as much as His words are heard.

However, this sensitivity must be balanced with obedience. Emotional engagement should never override your commitment to speak only what God has commanded. *"The secret of the Lord is with those who fear Him, and He will show them His covenant."* (Psalm 25:14) By guarding your heart and staying humble, you ensure that your emotions serve the message, not distract from it.

Why do prophets often feel isolated or misunderstood? It's because your emotional connection to God sets you apart. But this separation isn't a punishment—it's a privilege. It allows you to carry His heart in ways others cannot, ensuring that your words bring life, healing, and transformation.

Spiritual Insight

Prophets carry a unique grace that enables them to perceive and articulate God's will with clarity. This isn't just an ability; it is an intimate connection with God's heart that sets prophets apart. Many prophets wonder why they experience heightened awareness or why they receive revelations that others might overlook. This is because they are designed to function as divine "radar systems," detecting the will of heaven and delivering it to earth.

Through visions, dreams, and impressions, God unveils His plans to prophets, often showing them, what others cannot see. This can feel overwhelming, especially when these revelations seem ahead of their time. But remember, being ahead is part of the prophetic grace. God entrusts you with insight to prepare others for what is coming. The Lord Himself said, *"If there is a prophet among you, I, the Lord, make Myself known to him in a vision; I speak to him in a dream."* (Numbers 12:6)

Discernment and Accurate Revelation

Prophets are often puzzled by their ability to "sense" what others cannot. Whether it is deception in a conversation or the spiritual atmosphere of a room, their discernment is heightened. This grace allows prophets to distinguish between what is genuine and what is false, offering clarity in times of uncertainty. However, this heightened discernment is not just for observation—it is for action.

Jesus highlighted the tension prophets face, stating, *"A prophet is not without honor except in his own country and in his own house."* (Matthew 13:57) This means that even when a prophet is overlooked or misunderstood, their value remains unquestionable in God's eyes. Prophets are called to deliver accurate and timely revelations, ensuring that God's people have the clarity needed to act decisively.

Prophets often struggle with the weight of carrying truths that others may resist. Why do you feel compelled to speak even when it seems no one wants to listen? It's because your words are not your own—they belong to God. He has entrusted you to be His voice, ensuring that His will is communicated clearly, no matter the resistance. Accuracy isn't just about foretelling events; it's about delivering God's message in the right way, at the right time, for the right purpose.

Deliverance and Spiritual Restoration

Prophets are often drawn to brokenness. They are burdened by injustice, spiritual bondage, and anything that opposes God's order. This isn't a coincidence—it's part of their divine assignment. Prophets carry an anointing to bring deliverance and restoration, whether it's freeing individuals from addiction, breaking spiritual strongholds over families, or calling nations back to righteousness.

"By a prophet the Lord brought Israel out of Egypt, and by a prophet he was preserved." (Hosea 12:13) Prophets function as spiritual midwives, helping people birth freedom, restoration, and divine purpose. They are catalysts for change, reformers who restore God's order in the church and society. If you've ever felt drawn to advocate for the oppressed or confront societal corruption, it's because your prophetic nature compels you to align the world with God's design.

Prophets often feel deeply about issues others overlook. This is not a burden—it is their grace. They have been given the ability to see what is broken so you can help fix it. Prophets are not only a mouthpiece but also a vessel through which God's power flows to heal, restore, and transform.

Restoration of Spiritual Authority

Prophets are God's chosen vessels to restore spiritual authority in His church and call His people back to covenant with Him. They carry a divine mandate that extends beyond the walls of the church, influencing societal norms, values, and institutions. Whether in education, governance, business, or other spheres of influence, prophets are catalysts for the revival of moral and ethical standards, anchoring every area of life in God's righteousness.

The prophetic ministry is one of restoration and alignment. *"He will turn the hearts of the fathers to the children, and the hearts of the children to their fathers."* (Malachi 4:6) Through their obedience to God's voice, prophets realign hearts with His purposes, bringing order where chaos has taken root. Prophets are commissioned to restore what has been broken, realign what has been misplaced, and reignite the principles of God's kingdom in every realm of influence. In their obedience, they prepare the way for God's authority to reign supreme, ensuring that His will is done on earth as it is in heaven.

Magnet for Information

Prophets naturally attract information, drawing out details from God, people, and even the spiritual atmosphere, often without intending to. You may find that simply being in the presence of a true prophet compels you to share what you had not planned to reveal. Their role as divine conduits makes them attuned to both spoken and unspoken truths. However, discernment is vital, as not every supernatural encounter originates from God, and not all received information is from the Holy Spirit.

A prophet must carefully evaluate the origins of what they perceive, ensuring their heart remains guarded and their discernment sharp. When conflicting or unclear information arises—such as receiving mixed signals from someone seeking validation for a decision—it is essential to test the spirits behind the messages. The Holy Spirit is never the author of confusion, and prophets must anchor themselves in His peace and truth to navigate such moments effectively.

For deeper insights into hearing and discerning the voice of God with clarity, watch for my upcoming book *"How to Hear God's Voice,"* which provides practical guidance for sharpening this critical prophetic skill.

Discerning People's Heart

Prophets are naturally in tune with the emotional and spiritual states of those around them. This can feel like a blessing and a challenge. Why do you feel people's pain so deeply? Why are you moved by what others might dismiss? It's because your sensitivity is divinely designed. You are not just called to deliver God's words but to connect with His heart for His people.

This sensitivity, however, must be managed. Without proper training, you may find yourself overwhelmed by what you perceive. *"The spirits of the prophets are subject to the prophets."* (1 Corinthians 14:32) This means that while you receive these impressions, you have the authority to regulate and steward them. Prophets like Samuel needed guidance from Eli to discern God's voice, and so do you. Proper mentorship and spiritual discipline ensure you remain stable and effective.

Understanding people's hearts is not about exposing them; it's about leading them back to God. Your role is to use what you perceive to guide, comfort, and encourage, ensuring that those you minister to feel seen, valued, and drawn closer to God's love.

Combatting False Prophecy

The prophetic realm is one of both power and danger. Prophets often wonder why they encounter spiritual opposition or why the authenticity of their calling is questioned. The answer lies in the enemy's strategy: he seeks to discredit the prophetic office because of its vital role in advancing God's kingdom.

Jesus warned, *"For false christs and false prophets will rise and show great signs and wonders, to deceive, if possible, even the elect."* (Matthew 24:24) This warning is not just about others—it's a call for you to remain vigilant. Not every vision, dream, or impression comes from God. Prophets must cultivate discernment, anchoring themselves in the Word and the Holy Spirit to differentiate between divine revelation and counterfeit experiences.

Why does the enemy attack prophets so fiercely? It's because your words carry the power to shift atmospheres, redirect destinies, and tear down his plans. By staying rooted in Scripture and submitting every revelation to the Holy Spirit, you protect your ministry from deception. Your vigilance not only preserves the purity of your message but also ensures that God's people receive the truth they need to thrive.

GROWTH AREAS FOR PROPHETS

Managing Emotional Burdens

As a prophet, you carry the weight of spiritual realities that most people cannot see or comprehend. The revelations you receive often come with a burden that presses deeply on your heart and emotions. This is not a flaw; it is evidence of your alignment with God's heart. Elijah's despair after confronting the prophets of Baal serves as a poignant reminder that even great prophets can feel overwhelmed by their calling (1 Kings 19:4-8). God's response to Elijah—offering rest, sustenance, and a fresh encounter—teaches us that emotional burdens are not meant to be carried alone.

It is crucial to know when to disengage. Just as *the spirits of the prophets are subject to the prophets* (1 Corinthians 14:32), you have the authority to turn off the gift temporarily to maintain emotional stability. Not every insight requires immediate action, nor should every emotional weight be taken personally. Ecclesiastes 7:21 advises, *"Do not take to heart everything people say, lest you hear your servant cursing you."* This wisdom reminds prophets to filter what they pick up and avoid internalizing everything they perceive.

Developing Emotional Maturity

Your emotions, as a prophet, are deeply intertwined with the spiritual burdens and revelations you carry. You may feel God's joy, grief, or anger in almost overwhelming ways. Without emotional maturity, these intense feelings can lead to instability, frustration, or even withdrawal. Jesus exemplifies perfect emotional balance: He wept for Lazarus (John 11:35), showed righteous anger in the temple (John 2:15-17), and yet never lost sight of His mission.

To grow in emotional maturity, practice guarding your heart as Solomon advised: *"Keep your heart with all diligence, for out of it spring the issues of life."* (Proverbs 4:23) Surround yourself with wise mentors who can help you navigate the complexities of your emotions. Learn to process what you feel in God's presence, choosing joy and love even when the burden feels heavy. Worship, laughter, and intentional moments of gratitude can stabilize your heart, allowing you to function effectively despite the weight of your calling.

Struggles in Relationships

One of the challenges prophets often face is navigating relationships while managing their emotional intensity. The truth is, no one wants to feel like they are walking on eggshells around someone who seems emotionally unpredictable. When others are joyful, you may find yourself grieving over something God has revealed. When others are mourning, you might feel joy because of a promise God has shown you. This contrast, while part of the prophetic nature, can be hard for others to understand.

Referring again to 1 Corinthians 14:32, *"The spirit of the prophet is subject to the prophet."* That's why prophets must rely on channels of grace to help regulate their emotions. These tools, such as prayer, meditation, or even journaling, allow you to process and balance your feelings effectively. Personally, I have found meditation to be a powerful way to reset and realign my emotions.

It is also important to educate those close to you about your prophetic tendencies. Helping loved ones understand your unique nature fosters connection and reduces misunderstandings. For example, my wife understands many of my prophetic rhythms and allows me space to express them. However, this does not mean prophets have a free pass to be dismissive or say, *"This is just how I am."* Instead, use wisdom and humility to explain your nature in a way that fosters understanding and connection.

Finally, seek relationships and environments where you are accepted and celebrated, not merely tolerated. The prophetic journey can feel isolating at times, but being in spaces where your calling is understood and valued makes all the difference.

Avoiding Misinterpretation

The weight of your prophetic words carries great responsibility. Your words must align with God's truth, as misinterpretation can cause confusion, lead people astray, or erode the trust placed in your ministry. The sobering warning in *Jeremiah 23:25-32* highlights the profound consequences of prophetic missteps, emphasizing the need for precision and faithfulness in delivering God's message.

As a prophet, your first responsibility is to ensure that every revelation you receive is delivered clearly, accurately, and in the right context. This begins with submission. Always bring your revelations to trusted leaders and mentors for discernment and guidance. These individuals act as sounding boards, helping you avoid potential missteps and ensuring your words are rooted in truth.

Ground yourself in Scripture, which remains the ultimate litmus test for any prophetic message. No word should ever contradict the revealed Word of God. Pray fervently for clarity, seeking God's direction on the timing and manner of delivery for each message. Often, the *'when'* and *'how'* are just as important as the *'what'*.

Remember, prophetic accuracy is not merely about predicting future events—it is about reflecting God's character and His heart. Your words should carry His love, grace, and justice. The clarity and faithfulness of your message have the power to shape the spiritual trajectory of those who hear it. Approach your calling with humility and reverence, knowing that each word has the potential to bring life, transformation, and alignment with God's purposes. Let every message you deliver reflect His truth and be a testament to His glory.

Balancing Revelation with Application

Prophetic revelations are meant to bring action, but without practical application, they can remain dormant. As a prophet, your role is not just to reveal God's plans but to collaborate with others to see them fulfilled. Nehemiah exemplifies this balance by turning divine revelation into actionable steps, rebuilding the walls of Jerusalem with unity and purpose.

Work closely with apostles, pastors, and other leaders to develop actionable strategies that align with God's revelations. Discern the timing of your words, understanding that a premature revelation can cause confusion while a delayed one can hinder progress. Tailor your messages to the needs of your audience, ensuring that they inspire faith and obedience. Your calling is not complete when you speak; it is fulfilled when the church aligns with God's will and moves forward in His purposes.

Strengthening Humility

Humility is essential for sustaining your prophetic calling. The honor and recognition that often accompany your ministry can subtly lead to pride, which is the greatest enemy of spiritual growth.

Cultivate humility by regularly reflecting on the source of your gift. Remind yourself that your ability to hear and speak God's words is a grace, not a merit. Engage in acts of service that remind you of your dependence on God. Seek accountability from trusted leaders and invite feedback on your ministry. Above all, redirect any praise or accolades back to the One who deserves all glory. Humility not only preserves your integrity but also ensures that your ministry remains pure and impactful.

Speak Right (Prophesy)

Prophecy is a divine tool of creation, empowered to bring God's will into reality. Ezekiel's vision of the valley of dry bones demonstrates this truth. Faced with a lifeless army, Ezekiel was instructed by God to prophesy. As he spoke, life was restored to the bones, illustrating that the world is malleable to the prophetic word. Just as creation began with God's Word, prophecy carries the same power to shape, recreate, and transform according to His will.

As a prophet, you are called to partner with God in this creative process. While prayer seeks God's intervention, prophecy commands His will into existence. Your words, under His authority, have the power to call forth life from death and order from chaos. This creative authority, however, demands discipline. Your tongue must be guided by the Spirit, for careless or negative words can carry unintended consequences. Proverbs 18:21 reminds us, *"Death and life are in the power of the tongue, and those who love it will eat its fruit."* Speak with intention, aligning your declarations with God's purposes.

To wield this power effectively, focus on what God has revealed, not on present circumstances. Prophesy His promises and declare life where there is despair. The role of prophecy is not to reflect the visible but to manifest the unseen future that aligns with God's will. Cultivate the habit of speaking life, ensuring your words partner with His plans.

Word of Knowledge vs. Word of Wisdom

Prophets often receive the *"what"*—revelation about a matter—but not always the *"how,"* which requires wisdom to act on that knowledge. While prophets are naturally inclined to operate in the word of knowledge, apostles frequently carry the word of wisdom. However, knowing a problem does not automatically guarantee understanding or solutions. Without seeking divine guidance, prophets risk offering flesh-driven advice.

The story of Daniel highlights this distinction. Daniel not only received knowledge but also the divine ability to interpret and apply it: *"God gave them knowledge and skill in all literature and wisdom; and Daniel had understanding in all visions and dreams."* (Daniel 1:17) Knowledge alone is just information, but understanding transforms it into actionable insight, as emphasized in Proverbs 4:7: *"In all your getting, get understanding."*

To fulfill your role as a watchman effectively, seek God's interpretation and strategy for every revelation. Avoid assuming that seeing or perceiving automatically grants the correct solution. Practice observation, meditation, and inquiry, and discern whether you are operating in the Spirit or the flesh. Mature prophets clarify when their suggestions are individual opinions and collaborate with trusted leaders when necessary.

Avoiding Distractions

Distractions are a prophet's greatest enemy, dulling spiritual sensitivity and obstructing divine revelation. As God's watchmen, you are called to maintain unwavering focus, attuned to His voice and attentive to His subtle signals. In ancient times, watchers stood on walls, alert to the smallest movement. Similarly, you must remain vigilant, guarding against the mental, emotional, and social distractions that can pull you away from your assignment.

God often knocks to get your attention, as He says, *"Behold, I stand at the door and knock. If anyone hears My voice and opens the door, I will come in to him and dine with him."* (Revelation 3:20) Sometimes, this knock comes as a disruption—a sudden change in circumstances, like dishonor where there was once honor. Instead of reacting emotionally, pause and ask, *"Lord, what are You saying?"* These moments are invitations to deeper understanding, not inconveniences to dismiss.

I recall a time when disrespect from a venue's management could have derailed me emotionally, but by seeking God, I realized He was prompting a transition into our new building. Had I focused on complaining, I would have missed His direction entirely.

Distractions can often arise from overcommitment and a lack of rest. If you are not hearing clearly, it may be God's way of calling you to pause and recalibrate. Rest is not indulgence—it is spiritual alignment. As Habakkuk declared, *"I will stand my watch and set myself on the rampart, and watch to see what He will say to me."* (Habakkuk 2:1) Only in stillness can you discern His voice.

Stay focused, guard your heart from emotional noise, and prioritize time for prayer and meditation. Allow these times of stillness to sharpen your spiritual sensitivity and align your heart with His purpose.

Cultivating Patience and Compassion

As a prophet, your insight can make it tempting to push people toward immediate action, but your role is also to shepherd hearts. God's patience with Israel throughout history reveals the long-suffering nature of His love. *"The Lord is not slack concerning His promise...but is longsuffering toward us."* (2 Peter 3:9) Similarly, you must learn to convey God's words with grace, allowing people time to process and respond.

Practice patience by praying for those who struggle to understand or act on your revelations. Develop compassion by seeing people through God's eyes, recognizing their potential rather than their current limitations. Speak the truth in love, knowing that your delivery can either build or break trust. Patience and compassion are not signs of weakness but of spiritual maturity, enabling you to lead others toward God's purposes with care and wisdom.

Maintaining Integrity

Integrity is the bedrock of a prophet's ministry. Without it, even the most accurate revelations lose their impact. Prophets are entrusted with divine insight not for personal gain but to serve and edify God's people. Misusing this gift for selfish purposes, like 'insider trading' in the stock market, undermines the sacred trust placed in you.

As Paul teaches in 1 Corinthians 12, spiritual gifts are given *"for the profit of all."* This is why Elisha refused Naaman's gift, understanding that prophetic ministry is not transactional. Similarly, you must guard against exploiting revelations for personal advantage or recognition. Your gift is a tool for advancing God's Kingdom, not for self-promotion.

As a prophet, consistently evaluate your motives. Ask, *"Am I using this revelation to glorify God or myself?"* Integrity demands that you handle divine insights with humility, transparency, and responsibility. In a time when false prophets abound, your integrity will be the mark of your authenticity, ensuring that your ministry reflects the holiness of the One who called you. Let your life and words bring glory to God and trust to His people.

Intercession

Intercession is core to a prophet's ministry—a mandate to release the burdens you receive back to God. Each word, vision, or revelation you carry is not meant to weigh you down but to inspire you to stand in the gap. Prophets act as spiritual advocates, lending their favor with God on behalf of others. Through prayer, you plead, *"Lord, for my sake, have mercy on them."* This sacred role positions you as a bridge between heaven and earth, ensuring that God's plans are fulfilled and His people are shielded.

God often reveals warnings or blessings to prophets as an invitation to partner with Him. When He shows you impending judgment, it is an opportunity to intercede for mercy, just as Moses did for Israel. Likewise, when God reveals a promise, you are called to agree in prayer for its swift manifestation. As Amos 3:7 declares, *"Surely the Lord God does nothing, unless He reveals His secret to His servants the prophets."*

However, the enemy seeks to distract prophets from this vital task, often through offense or emotional overwhelm. Some burdens will lift quickly, while others require persistent prayer over months or even years. Let your intercession be unwavering, for it is through this that destinies are preserved, nations are transformed, and lives are redeemed.

Reading the Word

For a prophet, the written Word is not optional; it is essential. While it may be tempting to rely solely on real-time rhema—visions, dreams, or perception—the Bible must remain your primary foundation. Daniel's experience in Daniel 10:16-19 underscores this truth. Though overwhelmed by visions, he was strengthened by divine words spoken to him. Similarly, the Word of God rejuvenates and anchors you, ensuring your gift operates in alignment with His will.

There is a vital distinction between feeding yourself with the Word and seeking a word for others. The former nourishes your spirit; the latter burdens you with responsibility. Always prioritize your personal edification before ministering to others. As Jeremiah 20:9 reveals, *"His word was in my heart like a burning fire shut up in my bones."* Let this fire fuel your journey.

Prophets are naturally drawn to the drama of their supernatural experiences, but consistent reading and meditation on the Word will keep you grounded. Build a disciplined routine around Scripture, allowing it to balance and preserve your prophetic gift.

Predisposed Ideas and Strong Desires

Prophets must guard their hearts diligently, as strong personal desires can easily cloud or distort divine communication. While desires themselves are not inherently wrong—Scripture encourages us to *"ask, and you shall receive"*—unchecked desires can misalign a prophet's focus and lead to confusion. A fixation on specifics, like desiring a black chair, may seem trivial but can cause a prophet to misinterpret personal preferences as divine instruction. Instead, maintain openness, trusting God to fulfill needs in His way and time.

I have found it wise to wait for God to place the right desires in my heart, often confirmed through prophetic words or other approved sources. This ensures alignment with His will rather than my ambitions. The concept of 'manifestation,' as taught by the world, can manipulate prophetic gifts, making it crucial to ensure all desires align with God's purposes. We will give an account for every manifestation driven by our desires.

The Lord once revealed to me that a person truly surrendered to Him will only recognize a need after God has declared or fulfilled it. This reflects true contentment—wanting nothing beyond what Jesus has promised. Bishop

David Oyedepo captures this wisdom well: *"Whatever God cannot give me, I don't want; wherever God cannot take me, I don't want to get there."* As 1 Timothy 6:6 says, *"Godliness with contentment is great gain."*

Contentment extends beyond material things to include times, seasons, and divine purposes. Embracing it reduces the likelihood of prophetic deception, aligning you with God's timing and eliminating distractions. Jeremiah 17:9 warns us: *"The heart is deceitful above all things, and desperately wicked; who can know it?"* A heart surrendered to God is purified, disciplined, and clear. A content prophet hears God's voice with accuracy, avoiding the pitfalls of personal ambition, and remains steadfast in their divine calling.

Boldness

Prophets must boldly deliver God's messages, speaking the truth without fear of opposition or personal repercussions. Boldness is confidence that enables you to stand firm, knowing that you are not acting alone but as a vessel of the Almighty.

Equally important to boldness is the discipline to withhold information when necessary. Not everything a prophet perceives or hears is meant to be shared immediately—or at all. There are times when others may try to pressure or intimidate you into revealing what God has not released. This is why the Lord reminded Jeremiah, *"Do not be afraid of their faces, for I am with you to deliver you."* (Jeremiah 1:8) God's touch on Jeremiah's mouth symbolizes the divine authority given to speak only what is commanded, neither adding nor withholding out of personal fear or bias.

Prophets must always seek the Holy Spirit's guidance before sharing what they've received. Ask Him whether the information is meant to be shared, and if so, with whom and how. Remember that God reveals in parts; assuming you know the full picture can lead to error and even pride. Carefully managing divine revelation protects not only the integrity of the message but also the trust placed in you as a prophet. Discerning what to say, when to say it, and how to say it reflects a prophet's spiritual maturity and commitment to God's will

Pride

The respect and honor prophets receive can subtly tempt you toward pride. As a spiritual ambassador, the recognition that comes with representing God can inflate your ego if unchecked. Always redirect praise and glory to God, the true source of your gift.

Romans 12:3 urges, *"Do not think of yourself more highly than you ought."* Humility is not self-deprecation but an accurate understanding of your dependence on God. A prophet's effectiveness diminishes when pride creeps in. Stay teachable, acknowledge your limitations, and remember that every vision, word, or miracle comes from God.

Biblical Examples of Prophets

Jeremiah

Known as the *Weeping Prophet*, Jeremiah's ministry was one of immense emotional and spiritual depth. He conveyed God's messages of judgment and hope with such profound intensity that it often came at great personal cost. Despite rejection and persecution, Jeremiah's commitment to his divine calling never wavered. God's affirmation to him— *"Before I formed you in the womb I knew you; before you were born I sanctified you; I ordained you a prophet to the nations"* (Jeremiah 1:5)—underscores the divine intentionality of his life's work. Jeremiah's perseverance teaches prophets the necessity of faithfulness to God's word, even when it demands emotional and personal sacrifice. His unwavering integrity remains a blueprint for prophetic authenticity.

Elijah

Elijah's ministry demonstrated the unparalleled power and presence of God through miraculous acts and bold confrontations with evil. He stood unyielding against the prophets of Baal, calling Israel to repentance and reigniting the nation's faith in God. The promise in Malachi 4:5— *"Behold, I will send you Elijah the prophet before the coming of the great and dreadful day of the Lord"*—reveals the enduring impact of his ministry. Elijah's life highlights the courage required of prophets to confront societal corruption and call people back to righteousness, even in the face of overwhelming opposition. His reliance on God's provision and bold actions inspire prophets to stand firm in truth and power.

Deborah

As both a prophetess and judge, Deborah exemplified prophetic leadership that combined discernment, wisdom, and courage. Her role in orchestrating Israel's military victory under Barak showcases her ability to unite and inspire others to act on divine instruction. *"Now Deborah, a prophetess, the wife of Lapidoth, was judging Israel at that time."* (Judges 4:4) Deborah's ministry serves as a powerful reminder that prophetic leadership goes beyond foretelling—it involves strategic decision-making, bold action, and nurturing the spiritual and societal well-being of a nation. Her example calls prophets to lead with clarity, strength, and a deep trust in God's direction.

Agabus

In the New Testament, Agabus represents the continuity of the prophetic office in the early church. His precise foretelling of the famine during Claudius Caesar's reign and Paul's imprisonment provided timely guidance for believers. *"Then one of them, named Agabus, stood up and showed by the Spirit that there was going to be a great famine throughout all the world."* (Acts 11:28) Agabus's ministry reminds prophets of their role as watchmen, offering warnings and insights to prepare God's people for challenges. His life teaches the importance of accuracy, humility, and a deep connection to the Holy Spirit in delivering life-saving messages.

Jonah

Jonah's reluctant obedience led to one of the most remarkable revivals in biblical history. His message of repentance transformed the city of Nineveh, showcasing the power of God's mercy and the impact of prophetic obedience. *"So the people of Nineveh believed God, proclaimed a fast, and put on sackcloth, from the greatest to the least of them."* (Jonah 3:5) Jonah's story is a vivid reminder that prophets must yield to God's call, even when it challenges personal comfort or preferences. It also highlights God's willingness to use imperfect vessels to accomplish extraordinary works of grace and restoration.

Isaiah

Isaiah's ministry spanned prophecies of judgment and consolation, offering profound revelations about the coming Messiah and the ultimate restoration of Israel. His words continue to resonate through generations: *"Therefore the Lord Himself will give you a sign: Behold, the virgin shall conceive and bear a Son, and shall call His name Emmanuel."* (Isaiah 7:14) Isaiah's life and writings exemplify the depth and breadth of prophetic revelation, reminding prophets of the eternal significance of their words. His ministry inspires a commitment to deliver messages that not only confront but also comfort, offering hope and guidance for the future.

Samuel

Samuel's life stands as a testament to integrity and faithfulness in fulfilling God's purposes. From his childhood dedication to God to his role as a prophet, judge, and leader, Samuel's ministry shaped the course of Israel's history. His unwavering honesty is evident in his public declaration: *"Here I am. Witness against me before the Lord and before His anointed: Whose ox have I taken, or whose donkey have I taken, or whom have I cheated?"* (1 Samuel 12:3) Samuel's legacy teaches prophets the necessity of maintaining a spotless reputation, delivering God's messages without compromise, and guiding people with wisdom during times of significant transition.

Daniel

Daniel's prophetic ministry was marked by extraordinary wisdom and the ability to interpret dreams and visions. Serving under multiple kings, he navigated foreign courts with remarkable integrity while remaining faithful to God. *"As for these four young men, God gave them knowledge and skill in all literature and wisdom; and Daniel had understanding in all visions and dreams."* (Daniel 1:17) Daniel's life exemplifies how prophets can influence nations and leaders without losing their spiritual identity. His example encourages prophets to seek divine wisdom, remain steadfast in their convictions, and trust in God's provision when navigating complex or hostile environments.

4

The Evangelistic Office

INTRODUCTION TO THE EVANGELISTIC OFFICE

The Evangelistic Office is integral to the Five-Fold Offices, centered on spreading the Gospel and bringing people into the Kingdom of God. The primary role of an evangelist within the body of Christ is twofold: to win souls and to keep souls on fire. It's not enough to bring people to Christ; the work of an evangelist is to ensure that they remain energized, joyful, and excited about their faith. Their job is to ignite passion and help people stay connected to God. In the marketplace, the evangelist can be expected to get people to adopt an idea, a product or a service and to get them continually excited about that idea, product or service.

You can think of their role as "fishers and hunters." When you fish, you cast a wide net, reaching out to as many people as possible at once. When you hunt, you're focused and intentional, targeting individuals in a way that meets them where they are. Both approaches are vital in evangelism, and we must be ready to do both.

The evangelist's work is also about proclaiming and exclaiming. To proclaim is to broadcast the word of God or any message widely with simplicity. Creating something people do not know about can be frustrating, and the evangelistic office meets the need for divine announcement. While the apostle institutes divine order, the evangelist brings about divine proclamation. When a true evangelist takes hold of what you do, it will be announced. God placed the evangelist in the body of Christ to ensure that no one is hidden. When evangelists take their place in the body, everyone who needs to be seen is seen, and everyone who needs to be heard is heard. The evangelist is like a megaphone, a microphone, an audio speaker, etc. They accentuate and broadcast others' messages.

To exclaim is to infuse the message with energy and excitement, to give people a fun experience that draws them closer to Christ. It's about making any message come alive in a way that people can't ignore.

In simple terms, the evangelist's job is to sell ideas - and in this case we are focusing on the gospel. Think of it like selling a product, except in this case, we are selling Jesus. We are winning souls to Him. But it's not just about "making the sale"—it's also about getting people excited about what we've sold to them, about the life and hope they've received. This is how we keep souls on fire.

So, let me ask you: *How do you sell Jesus to others?* This is the challenge we must take up as evangelists. It's about presenting the gospel in a way that is compelling, relatable, and full of joy, so that the people we reach are inspired to take action and experience true transformation.

A Biblical Guide to Understanding the Evangelistic Gifting

In **Luke 2:8-20**, we see a beautiful and clear illustration of the evangelistic office through the story of the shepherds and the angel. The shepherds, who were faithfully watching over their flock by night, were suddenly visited by an angel of the Lord, and the glory of God shone around them. This divine encounter reflects the very nature of evangelism—bringing the glory and presence of God to others in a way that compels action, stirs excitement, and spreads the good news.

Luke 2:10 says, *"Then the angel said to them, 'Do not be afraid, for behold, I bring you good tidings of great joy which will be to all people.'"*

Evangelists are carriers of joy and good news. Their role is to proclaim the gospel with simplicity, clarity, and energy that reaches all people. Even when delivering warnings of judgment or hell, an evangelist ensures that hope is never absent. The focus remains on offering salvation, redemption, and transformation through Jesus Christ. Evangelists, like the angel, bring a message that is full of life: *"I bring you good tidings of great joy."*

Luke 2:11 says, *"For there is born to you this day in the city of David a Savior, who is Christ the Lord."*

The message of an evangelist is straightforward and Christ-centered. It does not require complex theological explanations or exhaustive doctrinal teachings. It is direct, accessible, and full of urgency. The angel's declaration highlights this simplicity: a Savior is born, and He is Christ the Lord. Similarly, an evangelist does not complicate the gospel; they focus on Jesus—the solution to sin, the hope of salvation, and the bringer of joy. Their role is to share this message boldly, ensuring it resonates with every listener.

Luke 2:15-16 continues, *"So it was, when the angels had gone away from them into heaven, that the shepherds said to one another, 'Let us now go to Bethlehem and see this thing that has come to pass, which the Lord has made known to us.' And they came with haste and found Mary and Joseph, and the Babe lying in a manger."*

This passage reveals the impact of a true evangelistic message. The shepherds' immediate and enthusiastic response shows the power of evangelism to compel people to act. Evangelists carry a voice of urgency—a God-given energy that motivates listeners to respond without hesitation. The shepherds did not delay or overanalyze the angel's proclamation; they acted *"with haste"* and found the Savior. In the same way, evangelists possess a compelling and clear message that stirs hearts and pushes people toward salvation.

Luke 2:17 highlights this ripple effect: *"Now when they had seen Him, they made widely known the saying which was told them concerning this Child."*

True evangelists do not stop at proclamation. They inspire others to share the message as well. The shepherds, having encountered the Savior, could not keep the good news to themselves. They *"made widely known"* what they had seen and heard, becoming evangelists. This is a hallmark of the evangelistic gifting: it multiplies. Evangelists not only proclaim the gospel but empower others to do the same, spreading the good news everywhere.

The Nature of Evangelistic Awakening

The story of the shepherds shows us that when evangelists are awake and active, they stir excitement, urgency, and transformation. Their presence brings life, movement, and an irresistible call to action. They remind the body of Christ that the gospel is too good to keep to ourselves. Evangelists are essential to the health and growth of the church, and their role must be celebrated and nurtured.

If you carry the evangelistic gifting, you must embrace your calling with boldness. Let your energy and passion drive you forward, spreading the message of salvation with joy and simplicity. Remember, the world needs the hope you carry. Just as the angel declared the good news with power and clarity, and the shepherds responded with urgency and excitement, so too are you called to awaken others to the reality of Jesus Christ.

CHARACTERISTICS OF AN EVANGELIST

Natural Persuader and Influencer

Evangelists carry a unique, God-given ability to influence and inspire action. Their words, presence, and passion compel others to embrace the Gospel with urgency and joy. This influence goes beyond mere words. It emanates from the evangelist's authenticity, conviction, and spiritual authority, stirring deep conviction in others and breaking barriers that keep hearts closed. Evangelists live with an infectious energy that motivates others to act—leading them toward salvation, healing, and hope.

If you feel your gift of persuasion has grown dormant, it's time to activate it. Begin where you are and with what you have. Share the Gospel with someone in your circle—whether it's a friend, a family member, or a colleague. Your influence might be expressed through public speaking, writing, music, or simple, heartfelt conversations. Ask the Holy Spirit to open doors and guide you to those ready to receive the message. Be prepared with a clear, simple testimony and a concise Gospel presentation, always ready to point others to Christ.

An evangelist thrives in motion. Act daily—whether through a personal conversation, an invitation to church, or even a post on social media. Small, intentional steps can create eternal impact. Influence is not neutral; it is always moving people toward something. As an evangelist, you are called to lead people toward God.

Gifted and Authentic Communicator

Evangelists excel in communication, speaking with intensity and conviction, often with little formal preparation. Their words flow naturally from the heart, driven by a divine compulsion to share the Gospel. As Paul charged Timothy: *"Preach the word! Be ready in season and out of season. Convince, rebuke, exhort with all longsuffering and teaching."* (2 Timothy 4:2)

What sets evangelists apart is their ability to simplify complex spiritual truths, making the Gospel relatable and accessible to everyone. They do not confuse their audience with deep theological concepts but focus on clarity and action. Their message carries an emotional weight that resonates with listeners, sparking transformation and motivating immediate responses.

Dynamic Energy and Enthusiasm

Energy is the hallmark of an evangelist. Whether they are speaking to a crowd, leading an outreach, or sharing one-on-one, evangelists bring life, excitement, and a contagious enthusiasm. This energy often replenishes naturally as they pour themselves into their work.

Philip's ministry again illustrates this dynamic power: *"The multitudes with one accord heeded the things spoken by Philip, hearing and seeing the miracles which he did."* (Acts 8:6) Evangelists carry a presence that makes people take notice. Even evangelists who express themselves quietly, such as music evangelists, have their unique energy style. They must resist the urge to compare themselves to others and instead embrace the grace God has given them.

Flexibility and Spontaneity

Evangelists thrive in dynamic, unstructured environments where they can move and adjust as God directs them. Their motion often creates direction, even when the way forward is not entirely clear. As Ecclesiastes 11:1 says, *"Cast your bread upon the waters, for you will find it after many days."*

Evangelists do not wait for exhaustive plans or perfect conditions—they act, trusting God to guide them as they go. Overplanning can stifle their effectiveness and suppress the spontaneity that makes their ministry so impactful. To remain in their element, evangelists should structure life to allow for flexibility (70-80%), leaving room for the Holy Spirit to lead them. This ability to adapt and pivot ensures their message remains fresh, relevant, and far-reaching.

Strong Faith That Produces Results

Evangelists operate with a profound level of faith. This faith is essential for seeing tangible results—salvations, miracles, and signs that confirm the Word they preach. *"Unclean spirits, crying with a loud voice, came out of many who were possessed; and many who were paralyzed and lame were healed."* (Acts 8:7)

Their faith allows them to take on large-scale evangelistic missions with boldness, trusting God for provision, guidance, and supernatural outcomes. This unwavering confidence enables evangelists to press forward even in the face of challenges, knowing that God's power accompanies their calling.

Exhorter and Encourager

The heart of an evangelist is to inspire and uplift. They are natural exhorters, calling people to action with messages that are both stirring and hopeful. Jesus said, *"The Spirit of the Lord is upon Me, because He has anointed Me to preach the gospel to the poor..."* (Luke 4:18) Even when delivering warnings, an evangelist always offers hope—pointing to the opportunity for redemption and transformation through Christ.

Strong Grace for Virality

Evangelists possess the natural ability to spread a message widely and rapidly. Like the Samaritan woman at the well, who invited her entire community to meet Jesus by saying, *"Come, see a Man who told me all things that I ever did..."* (John 4:29), evangelists create momentum that draws others in. Their testimonies and proclamations resonate deeply, leading people to share the message further. This grace for "virality" makes evangelists catalysts for revival and widespread Gospel impact.

Project-Focused and Action-Oriented

While apostles often move across various domains, evangelists are typically project-focused. They pour their energy into specific campaigns, events, or outreach missions, ensuring these projects are carried through to completion. Philip's focus on Samaria illustrates this: *"He went down to the city of Samaria and preached Christ to them."* (Acts 8:5)

Evangelists have an intense determination to see the work completed. Their focused approach ensures measurable results and sustained impact in their evangelistic efforts.

Desirable and Attractive

The grace of God on an evangelist's life makes what they offer deeply attractive. Their connection to the Gospel message, and their ability to communicate it persuasively, draws people in. Evangelists create emotional and spiritual connections, presenting the Gospel as the answer people need—making it irresistible to those who are searching for truth, hope, and joy.

Joyful and Positive

Evangelists are carriers of good news and joy. Regardless of challenges, they focus on the message of hope and redemption. Even when delivering difficult truths, they frame it with positivity: *"You don't have to go to hell;*

you can receive Jesus." Their optimism brings light into darkness, reflecting the joy of salvation.

GROWTH AREAS FOR EVANGELISTS

Believing the Lie That You Are "Doing Too Much"

One of the devil's most subtle tactics against evangelists is convincing you that you're "too much"—too loud, too intense, or too passionate. These are all lies from the pit of hell. Your energy, your boldness, and your passion are not flaws; they are gifts given by God to fulfill your calling. If you reduce your intensity to please others, you are handcuffing yourself and silencing the very gift that was meant to shake the world.

I've seen it happen—evangelists who once carried vibrant energy and an unmistakable voice have started to shrink back. Someone told you, *"You're too much. Tone it down."* And you believed it. You started to quiet yourself, dim your light, and blend in. But let me tell you the truth: you were designed to stand out. If you're not "doing too much," you're probably not doing enough.

When someone shouts in a crowd, everyone turns to look. That's how you were designed. You were built to draw attention—not to yourself, but to the message of Christ. Your energy, your passion, and your intensity are tools God uses to capture hearts and stir people to action. The enemy knows this, which is why he attacks it. He uses people with insecurities to project their limitations onto you but do not listen to them.

You have permission to be bold. You have permission to be loud. You have permission to do "too much." That's what God designed you for. Your voice should be heard. Your energy should turn heads. Your passion should inspire action. Don't let the enemy silence you, and don't let the opinions of others dictate your purpose.

Impatience for Results and Overcoming Spiritual Contention

Evangelists, with their passion and high energy, often expect quick and visible results when sharing the Gospel. Their natural enthusiasm drives them to push for immediate change, and when results are delayed, it can lead to frustration and discouragement. Paul's counsel to Timothy serves as a powerful reminder: *"Preach the word! Be ready in season and out of season. Convince, rebuke, exhort with all long-suffering and teaching."* (2 Timothy 4:2) This verse highlights the need for patience and perseverance, even when it seems like nothing is happening. Evangelists must remember that delayed results are not a reflection of the power they carry. The anointing on their lives and the transformative power of the Gospel remain undiminished, even when the harvest is not immediately visible.

The enemy, recognizing the significance of the evangelist's calling, works tirelessly to hinder their influence. This spiritual contention causes resistance and delays in people taking action, even after hearing the message. The enemy does not contend with efforts that have no impact; opposition is confirmation that your work is disrupting his plans. Evangelists must approach these challenges with a spiritual mindset, knowing they are fighting a battle far greater than what can be seen in the natural.

By separating results from their identity, evangelists can remain focused on their mission. Delayed results do not define their success, nor do they diminish the authority and energy God has given them. Instead, these challenges serve as an opportunity to deepen their trust in God and continue proclaiming the Gospel with boldness, knowing that their labor is never in vain. Evangelists must remember that their faithfulness, not visible outcomes, is the mark of a successful ministry.

Keep the Message Simple and Partner with Teachers

Evangelists thrive when they keep their message simple, clear, and focused on Christ. The power of the Gospel lies in its simplicity—not in complicated theological arguments. Your role is to stir hearts, awaken faith, and inspire immediate action—not to drown your audience in complexity.

There will always be pressure to sound more "deep" or match the teaching styles of pastors and teachers. Resist it. That's not your lane. The message of the evangelist is meant to be direct and to the point: *"For there is born to you this day... a Savior, who is Christ the Lord."* (Luke 2:11) This kind of clarity moves people to respond, and that's where your strength lies. Don't lose the edge of your calling by trying to be something you're not.

At the same time, you don't have to do it all alone. Partner with teachers who can build on the foundation you've laid. While you bring people into the kingdom with fire and conviction, teachers help ground them in the truth, ensuring they grow deep roots. This partnership is powerful—evangelists bring people to Christ, and teachers disciple them in His Word.

Guarding and Generating Energy

Evangelists are called to carry joy and energy, but to sustain this calling, they must learn to guard and intentionally generate the energy they need. Your energy is not limitless; what you pour into others must be replenished. Without intentional care, you risk burnout, discouragement, and ineffectiveness.

Physical Energy

Treat your body as the vehicle for your calling. Discover the foods, rest, and physical activities that energize you. The Holy Spirit can guide you on what works for your body. If you neglect your health, your message will suffer. Strengthen your temple so you can carry the fire of your assignment.

Mental and Emotional Energy

Guard your mind. Avoid negativity and environments that drain you. Surround yourself with joyful, encouraging people. As Galatians 5:22 reminds us, *"The fruit of the Spirit is love, joy, peace."* Joy is not laughter alone but a decision to carry an atmosphere of hope. Protect your peace, and change your environment if it pulls you down.

Spiritual Energy

Your energy flows from your connection with God. Prayer, worship, and meditation on His Word are non-negotiable. Never neglect your time with God. You cannot distribute energy to others if you are not receiving it first from Him. A dry spirit produces a dry message, but when you are full, you will overflow into the lives of those you minister to.

Battling Depression and Isolation

Evangelists are often the life of the room—the ones who bring joy, energy, and encouragement wherever they go. But what happens when the room is empty? For many evangelists, the contrast between their public persona and private struggles can be overwhelming. After pouring themselves out for others—cracking jokes, stirring energy, and spreading hope—they return home to silence, battling feelings of emptiness, depression, and isolation. This isn't just a story; it's a real and profound battle.

This struggle is a form of spiritual warfare. The same person who brings smiles to the world can sit alone in darkness, asking, *"Why am I even here?"* This is the enemy's calculated attack on your purpose. The devil knows your energy, your voice, and your passion carry the power to lead multitudes to Christ. His strategy is to isolate you—mentally, emotionally, and spiritually—hoping to silence the very gift God has placed within you.

But you matter, and your gift matters. God did not call you to bring joy to others while you remain trapped in despair. He placed a divine energy within you, an energy meant to shine—not just for others, but for you as well. When you embrace who you are and the grace God has given you, the chains of depression and isolation begin to break.

To overcome this, stay connected to God through prayer, worship, and His Word. Surround yourself with people who uplift you and remind you of your worth. When lies threaten your spirit, counter them with truth: *"You are the light of the world. A city set on a hill cannot be hidden."* (Matthew

5:14) Recognize the enemy's tactics and fight back with the strength of community and intentional action.

You are not alone in this battle. God sees you, values you, and sustains you. He has called you for a purpose, and He will equip you to fulfill it. Step boldly into the fullness of your identity as an evangelist, knowing you are meant to shine brightly—even when darkness tries to close in.

Intentional Influence

Your energy as an evangelist naturally draws people and moves them to action. But the question is: where are you leading them? Influence is not neutral. It is always moving people in a direction. As Paul reminds us, *"All things are lawful... but not all things edify."* (1 Corinthians 10:23)

Every word, post, conversation, and action sends a message. Are you pointing people to Christ, or are you leading them toward distractions? Your influence is a responsibility. If you are not intentional, you are wasting it.

How are you using your influence today? Are you stirring faith, hope, and purpose, or are you focused on things with no eternal value? God gave you this boldness and energy to transform lives. Don't let it be diluted. Use your influence to shift atmospheres, ignite purpose, and draw people into God's kingdom.

Integrity in Evangelism

Evangelists carry a powerful gift of persuasion, a God-given ability to move people toward action. However, this gift must always be rooted in integrity and truth. Paul exhorted believers, *"Let each of you speak truth with his neighbor, for we are members of one another."* (Ephesians 4:25) Integrity is not optional—it is the foundation that builds trust, credibility, and lasting impact in ministry.

The temptation to embellish or exaggerate stories for greater effect can be subtle, but dangerous. Without proper spiritual guidance, the line between persuasion and manipulation can blur. Evangelists must be careful that their zeal for conversions does not compromise the purity of their message. As Paul noted, *"They have a zeal for God, but not according to knowledge."* (Romans 10:2) Enthusiasm and passion are essential, but they must be balanced with truth and wisdom.

True evangelism does not rely on emotional manipulation or sensationalism. It rests on the power of the Gospel alone. Remember, the results are God's responsibility; your role is to deliver His message with honesty and integrity. When you speak truthfully and authentically, you allow the Holy Spirit to work in people's hearts, producing genuine transformation.

Managing Impulsiveness and Staying Committed

Evangelists are naturally driven by enthusiasm, joy, and passion, which are essential for their calling. However, this high-energy nature can sometimes lead to impulsiveness and unfinished projects. While evangelists often operate on motivation and excitement, ministry cannot depend on emotions alone.

To avoid impulsiveness and inconsistency, evangelists benefit greatly from accountability and partnership with other ministry offices, especially apostles. Apostles bring strategic oversight, helping to anchor the evangelist's zeal within a broader vision. This partnership ensures their energy is directed toward well-planned initiatives that produce lasting results. Finally, evangelists must remain grounded in *"the joy of the Lord"* (Nehemiah 8:10). Joy provides the strength and stability needed to stay focused and committed, regardless of circumstances.

Owning Your Evangelistic Gift

Evangelists often underestimate their gift, dismissing it as mere energy or enthusiasm. *"It's just energy. What am I supposed to do with this?"* But that energy has the power to change nations and transform lives. Look at figures like Donald Trump—regardless of opinions, his influence and boldness mirror the energy of an evangelist.

One of the greatest traps evangelists face is comparison. Many feel pressure to act like teachers, pastors, or apostles because they perceive those roles as more stable or respected. This comparison can lead to frustration and a rejection of their true calling. But God does not give "lesser" gifts. Your boldness, energy, and ability to stir hearts are not flaws—they are intentional tools God has placed within you to advance His Kingdom.

Stop comparing yourself to others or downplaying your gift in search of something "better." Walk boldly in the grace God has given you. Your energy, passion, and voice are exactly what this world needs. Embrace your evangelistic gift with confidence, knowing that God has uniquely equipped you to reach people in ways no one else can.

BIBLICAL EXAMPLES OF EVANGELISTS

Philip

Philip stands out as one of the clearest examples of an evangelist in the New Testament. His ministry in Samaria demonstrates the transformative power of evangelistic outreach. Philip preached Christ boldly, leading many to salvation and confirming the message with miraculous signs and wonders. *"Then Philip went down to the city of Samaria and preached Christ to them."* (Acts 8:5) Philip's ability to share the Gospel with urgency and clarity brought great joy to the city, showing the impact of a Spirit-filled evangelist.

Paul

Though primarily an apostle, Paul's evangelistic zeal is undeniable. He traveled extensively, preaching the Gospel to diverse audiences and planting churches. What set Paul apart was his ability to adapt the message of Christ to reach people from all walks of life. His words echo the heart of an evangelist: *"I have become all things to all people so that by all possible means I might save some."* (1 Corinthians 9:22) Paul's example highlights the importance of flexibility, cultural awareness, and a relentless desire to reach the lost.

The Samaritan Woman

The Samaritan woman's encounter with Jesus at the well turned her into an instant evangelist. Her testimony—simple, heartfelt, and personal—drew her entire community to Christ. She said, *"Come, see a Man who told me all things that I ever did. Could this be the Christ?"* (John 4:29) Her story reveals that evangelism does not require theological complexity but rather a willingness to share one's personal experience with Jesus. The curiosity she sparked led many to believe, proving that anyone transformed by Christ can evangelize effectively.

The Madman of Gadara

Delivered from torment and transformed by Jesus, the hitherto madman of Gadara became a powerful voice for the Gospel. Jesus told him, *"Go home to your friends and tell them what great things the Lord has done for you, and how He has had compassion on you."* (Mark 5:19) He obeyed and proclaimed the good news throughout Decapolis, and *"all marveled."* (Mark 5:20) His story illustrates the power of personal testimony and how sharing one's deliverance can draw others to Christ. It also reminds evangelists that God can use anyone—regardless of their past—to spread the message of salvation.

The Walls of Jericho

The story of Jericho's walls falling is a powerful symbol of raw evangelistic energy. The Israelites' collective shouting, as commanded by God, released a breakthrough that human strategy could not achieve. This demonstrates the evangelist's ability to channel bold, energetic, and faith-filled expressions to tear down spiritual barriers and usher in victory. When evangelists move in obedience, their voice becomes a tool to break strongholds and bring others into the freedom of Christ.

5

The Pastoral Office

INTRODUCTION TO THE PASTORAL OFFICE

The pastoral office is one of profound importance and service, yet it is often misunderstood. Many who struggle to locate themselves within the Five-Fold ministry might discover their identity in the pastoral grace. Pastors, like apostles, are generalists—a unique blend of all the other offices. Think of them as spiritual general practitioners, much like family doctors in the medical field, who are equipped to diagnose, guide, and refer individuals to specialized care. This design is intentional and vital, ensuring the congregation receives holistic care.

Pastors carry traces of the apostolic for oversight, the prophetic for discernment, the evangelistic for outreach, and the teaching grace to nourish and instruct. This broad capacity positions them to fill gaps and strengthen the body of Christ in every area, playing a foundational role in God's work. As Paul highlights:

"And God has appointed these in the church: first apostles, second prophets, third teachers, after that miracles, then gifts of healings, helps, administrations, varieties of tongues. Are all apostles? Are all prophets? Are all teachers? Are all workers of miracles?" (1 Corinthians 12:28-30)

The Calling of a Pastor

Pastors carry unique gifts that set them apart, including helps, administration, and the ability to connect deeply with people. This is not a skill learned by chance; it's a divine grace that enables them to speak the "language" of people. While others may struggle to relate or communicate across diverse groups, pastors transcend these barriers with ease, ensuring no one feels unseen or unheard.

Have you ever wondered why some people naturally offend others when trying to communicate? It is because they do not carry the pastoral grace. Pastors, however, are gifted at breaking down walls, connecting authentically, and bringing clarity where there was once misunderstanding. They speak to the heart of individuals, not just their minds, creating bonds that reflect the care of Christ Himself.

A Biblical Guide to Understanding the Pastoral Gifting

The essence of the pastoral office is beautifully illustrated in Psalms 23, a passage that reflects God as the ultimate shepherd. If you seek to understand and grow in the pastoral grace, this Psalm is a divine blueprint.

Psalms 23:1, *"The Lord is my Shepherd; I shall not want."*

This powerful declaration of faith by David is a timeless reminder that when the Lord is your pastor, you will lack nothing. The term "pastor" is synonymous with "shepherd" or "overseer," emphasizing care, guidance, and provision.

Is the Lord truly your shepherd? Are you submitting to His guidance? When you do, you can confidently proclaim that you will never lack any good thing because your care is in the hands of the ultimate Pastor. God's capacity to provide for His children is boundless and eternal. His provision is not limited by time, space, or need—it is infinite and ever-sufficient.

Psalms 23:2, *"He makes me to lie down in green pastures..."*

A pastor creates environments of peace and growth, leading their flock to places of spiritual nourishment and rest. Wherever a pastor's anointing is present, strife cannot thrive, and confusion is replaced with clarity. This grace ensures the church remains a sanctuary of order and abundance.

Psalms 23:3, *"He restores my soul; He leads me in the paths of righteousness for His name's sake."*

One thing you find in pastoral ministry is the restoration of the soul and proper guidance. A true shepherd leads people toward righteousness, but do you know that you can unknowingly mislead people? That is why Paul told Timothy, *"Study to show yourself approved..."* (2 Timothy 2:15) Pastors must ensure that they are well-educated so they are not leading people based on their intentions but in the direction of God's desires.

Psalms 23:4, *"Yea, though I walk through the valley of the shadow of death, I will fear no evil; For You are with me..."*

No matter who your pastor is, there will be times when you must walk through the valley of the shadow of death. This assurance reminds us that we are never alone, even in the darkest seasons.

When you first start walking with God, you might think challenges won't come your way. But as you mature, you'll understand that valleys—those seasons of shadows and difficulty—are no respecter of persons. They come to everyone. However, as Christians, we don't live through ups and downs;

we experience seasons of sowing and reaping. What may seem like a dark time is often just a season of sowing, a time of preparation for a bountiful harvest.

If you misinterpret those moments, the enemy will use them to discourage and derail you. But when you view them correctly, you'll see they are opportunities to celebrate God's faithfulness and press into His presence. Every season has its purpose, and even the dark times can yield benefits if approached with faith and wisdom. Use those moments to draw closer to God, build resilience, and prepare for the blessings He has ahead.

Verse 4 continues, saying, *"Your rod and Your staff, they comfort me."*

The rod and staff of the shepherd symbolize divine guidance and protection. The rod represents authority and correction, used to steer and direct the sheep onto the right path, especially in dark and challenging times. The staff, on the other hand, is a tool of support and rescue, a reassuring presence that brings comfort in moments of uncertainty.

When life feels overwhelming, the rod and staff become essential. These guiding principles anchor us, ensuring we stay aligned with God's will, even when everything around us feels unstable. During such times, it's vital to lean into these tools, allowing them to bring clarity, discipline, and peace.

Psalms 23:5, *"You prepare a table before me in the presence of my enemies..."*

Let's talk about enemies—I love enemies! There are lessons and opportunities only enemies can bring, making them essential for growth and progress. Good friends often shy away from delivering the tough truths you need to hear because they want to encourage and uplift you. But enemies? They'll tell you the hard truths without hesitation. Their opposition can become the very catalyst that propels you to the next level.

However, you cannot truly appreciate the value of enemies if you are emotionally fragile. The reality is, no amount of fasting or praying will eliminate enemies from your life. They are a part of God's divine design for sharpening and strengthening you. That's why God Himself prepares a table for you in their presence—not away from them, but right before their eyes. It's His way of demonstrating that their efforts to bring you down will only elevate you further.

This verse also reminds us that battles should never prevent us from enjoying life. Even in the midst of opposition, God calls us to thrive, grow, and expand. The presence of enemies doesn't diminish God's provision or His blessings over your life. Instead, it becomes the backdrop for His abundant favour, showing that no scheme of the enemy can stop His purpose for you. Let the table God prepares be a celebration of His power to elevate you, even in the face of adversity.

The same verse continues to say, *"You anoint my head with oil; my cup runs over."*

I once heard a man of God ask, *"Why does the cup run over? Isn't that waste?"* According to him, God responded, *"I just want to show you that I have more than enough."*

This principle is especially evident in pastoral ministry. When God anoints, He equips not only for sufficiency but for overflow, ensuring that the blessings in your life spill over to impact others. All of this happens within the church's framework. This is why belonging to a local church is so vital. The anointing, the overflow, and the communal blessings God has designed for His people are best experienced in the context of spiritual family. No matter who you are, being rooted in a church allows you to walk in the fullness of God's provision and participate in the overflow He desires for your life.

Psalms 23:6, *"Surely goodness and mercy shall follow me all the days of my life; And I will dwell in the house of the Lord forever."*

You should never expect things in your life to get worse, the Bible says *"the path of the just is like a shining star that shines ever brighter unto the perfect day."* (*Proverbs 4:18*) Follow the steps, apply divine principles and watch the goodness of God follow you all the days of your life.

Characteristics of a Pastor

Servant Leader

Pastors are divinely built for service, carrying the very heart of Christ in their leadership. They prioritize the needs of their flock above their own, serving with humility, empathy, and unwavering devotion. To a true pastor, service is not a chore; it is a sacred privilege, a reflection of the love and care of the Great Shepherd. Jesus Himself said, *"But he who is greatest among you shall be your servant."* (Matthew 23:11)

A pastor does not see their leadership as a platform for power but as an opportunity to pour into others, guiding and inspiring them to grow into all God has called them to be. This servant-driven mindset shines in every act of care, whether in comforting the weary, correcting the lost, or celebrating victories. Even beyond the church, this heart for service translates powerfully into leadership roles where uplifting and motivating others is key.

Pastors are called to mirror Christ in every way, serving tirelessly and faithfully, knowing that their labor is not in vain.

Balanced Vessel of Ministry

Pastors are uniquely graced to embody a divine balance, seamlessly blending aspects of the apostolic, prophetic, evangelistic, and teaching offices. This God-given versatility equips them to address the diverse and multifaceted needs of their flock, ensuring that no soul is left uncared for and no area is neglected. Paul captures this divine design when he writes: *"And He*

Himself gave some to be apostles, some prophets, some evangelists, and some pastors and teachers." (Ephesians 4:11)

A true pastor fills the gaps where other offices may fall short, acting as a stabilizing force within the body of Christ. While the evangelist ignites the fire, the pastor tends to it, ensuring it burns steadily. While the apostle charts new territories, the pastor grounds and nurtures those entrusted to their care. This ability to bring balance and harmony is not merely a skill but a reflection of God's heart for His people.

Their multifaceted grace extends beyond the church walls, making pastors invaluable in areas like project management and administration, where diverse skills are needed to coordinate and sustain success. Pastors don't just manage tasks—they shepherd people, bringing order, unity, and care to any environment they serve.

Shepherd Who Provides Compassionate Guidance

Pastors excel in providing compassionate guidance that prioritizes the well-being and growth of their congregation. With understanding and care, they lead individuals toward spiritual and personal maturity, helping them navigate life's challenges while remaining deeply rooted in faith. Like a shepherd who knows their sheep deeply, pastors ensure no one feels forgotten or left behind. Jesus Himself demonstrated this care, saying, *"I am the good shepherd. The good shepherd lays down his life for the sheep."* (John 10:11)

This role goes beyond the pulpit. Whether in ministry, counselling, social work, or leadership, pastors are uniquely equipped to guide others with wisdom and compassion, bringing out the best in them. God promises in

His Word, *"And I will give you shepherds according to My heart, who will feed you with knowledge and understanding."* (Jeremiah 3:15)

Under the right pastoral care, lives are transformed. Growth is inevitable when someone walks under the covering of a pastor who knows how to feed their spirit, guard their soul, and inspire their mind. While evangelists ignite passion and prophets bring divine revelation, pastors provide the ongoing care that keeps believers rooted, sustained, and thriving. Pastors carry the grace to shepherd people for decades without growing weary, ensuring they are equipped and grounded for life's journey.

Healing

Pastors are vessels of God's divine power, uniquely graced to facilitate holistic healing across all dimensions of human existence—physical, mental, emotional, and spiritual. Their role extends beyond spiritual care to addressing the full spectrum of an individual's well-being, ensuring a comprehensive restoration that aligns with God's design for wholeness.

James 5:14 emphasizes their active role in healing: *"Is anyone among you sick? Let him call for the elders of the church, and let them pray over him, anointing him with oil in the name of the Lord."* This highlights their responsibility to intercede, anoint, and shepherd others toward divine health.

Pastors create environments where healing is not merely an act but an ongoing process involving prayer, teaching, and practical care. They address physical ailments through faith and intercession, emotional wounds through encouragement and reassurance, mental struggles through wise counsel, and spiritual brokenness by guiding individuals back to God's promises.

This capacity for holistic healing equips pastors to impact lives within and beyond the church. In professions such as medicine, wellness, and caregiving, their understanding of restoration becomes invaluable for guiding individuals toward recovery and renewed strength. Pastors don't just treat symptoms—they address root causes, bringing people into alignment with God's perfect will for their lives.

Support in Restoration of Souls

Pastors provide emotional and spiritual support, aiding in the restoration of those who are broken or weary. They offer healing through counsel and encouragement, helping individuals to recover and grow in their faith. Their support is a source of strength for anyone needing comfort and guidance. *"He makes me to lie down in green pastures; He leads me beside still waters. He restores my soul..."* (Psalms 23:2-3) This supportive role is crucial in fields such as mental health, therapy, and nursing, where individuals require consistent care and restoration.

Pastors are God's chosen vessels for bringing emotional and spiritual restoration to the broken and weary. They offer more than just guidance; they create environments of healing through prayer, counsel, and heartfelt encouragement. Their presence carries a calming reassurance that allows people to confront their struggles, release their pain, and find renewed strength in God's promises.

This restorative work is deeply emotional, meeting people in their most vulnerable places and guiding them toward wholeness in Christ. Pastors do not just address symptoms; they minister to the heart, nurturing growth, and rebuilding faith. Whether within the church or in professions like therapy, nursing, and caregiving, pastors are agents of God's healing, equipping individuals to rise from their weariness and walk confidently in their God-given purpose.

Guardian of the Flock

Pastors are vigilant shepherds, entrusted by God to shield His people from spiritual danger. They stand watch, discerning false teachings, negative influences, and anything that threatens the purity and safety of the flock. Their unwavering commitment ensures a spiritually healthy and secure environment where believers can thrive. Jesus spoke of this protective role, warning against neglectful leaders who abandon their charge: *"The hireling, who is not the shepherd, sees the wolf coming and leaves the sheep and flees."* (John 10:12)

True pastors do not flee when challenges arise. They confront threats head-on, willing to sacrifice for the sake of the flock's well-being. This calling extends beyond the church walls into roles like education and child-care, where safeguarding and nurturing individuals are equally essential. Pastors are protectors at heart, standing firm to ensure those under their care remain grounded in truth and shielded from harm.

Protector and Caregiver

Pastors have a natural ability to protect and care for those under their responsibility, ensuring their safety and well-being. This caregiving aspect of the pastoral role involves nurturing, safeguarding, and providing for the congregation's physical, emotional, and spiritual needs. *"He will flock his flock like a shepherd; He will gather the lambs in His arm, and carry them in his bosom, and gently lead those who are with young."* (Isaiah 40:11) In fields like healthcare, elder care, and hospitality, this trait is vital for creating safe and supportive environments.

When the devil often wants to take advantage of people, he isolates them from their shepherd. As pastors, we have been charged with caring for God's children, so what we do is extremely important. It goes beyond the excuse of being shy. Sometimes, it is as simple as a phone call or a text to check up on people. God did not say we must forcefully bring people back, but He values the effort in our pursuit. The reality is that we cannot force or control people to follow us. Our job is to tirelessly extend love, mercy, compassion, and care, regardless of the response. God gave pastors as an extension of His care for us.

Intimate Knowledge of their Congregation

Pastors get to know their congregants deeply, understanding their individual needs, strengths, and challenges. This intimate knowledge allows pastors to provide personalized ministry, address specific issues and help individuals grow in their walk with God. *"I am the good shepherd; I know my sheep and my sheep know me."* (John 10:14) This trait is equally valuable in roles such as personal counselling, human resources, and any position that requires a deep understanding of individual needs for effective mentorship and support.

Pastors are entrusted with a profound responsibility to know their flock intimately. They are not distant leaders but compassionate shepherds who recognize the unique needs, strengths, and challenges of everyone under their care. This deep connection enables them to minister with precision, offering guidance that meets people where they are and helping them grow in their faith journey.

This divine insight is not limited to spiritual leadership but extends into roles like counselling, human resources, and mentorship—positions that demand personalized care and wisdom. Pastors are conduits of God's love, shaping lives through their understanding and ensuring each person feels seen, valued, and supported on their path to wholeness.

Build Deep Connection

Pastors carry a divine grace to connect deeply with individuals, offering tailored guidance and unwavering support. They are tuned into the unique needs of each person in their care, creating safe spaces for vulnerability and trust. This ability reflects the heart of Jesus, who said, *"I know My sheep, and am known by My own."* (John 10:14) Pastors are not just leaders but shepherds who walk closely with their flock, ensuring that no one feels overlooked. This skill is essential in roles like mentorship, counselling, and leadership, where personal connection is the foundation for transformation.

Emotionally Intelligent

Pastors embody the heart of Christ through their deep emotional intelligence, a gift that allows them to sense and respond to the unspoken needs of those they shepherd. They are not just compassionate but also discerning, knowing when to offer encouragement, when to challenge, and when to simply listen. Paul's exhortation captures this relational grace: *"Bear one another's burdens, and so fulfill the law of Christ."* (Galatians 6:2)

Their ability to navigate complex emotions and foster meaningful connections equips them to minister effectively to those in pain, offering comfort and clarity in moments of distress. This divine sensitivity extends beyond ministry into roles like counselling, social work, and mediation, where understanding and addressing emotional needs is key. A pastor's relational gift is not merely about empathy but about healing, guiding, and empowering others to embrace the fullness of life in Christ.

Unifier of Communities

Pastors are anointed to foster unity within the body of Christ, creating communities where every individual feels valued and connected. They draw people together, overcoming differences and promoting harmony in ways that mirror the early church: *"Now all who believed were together, and had all things in common."* (Acts 2:44) Their ability to build a sense of belonging extends beyond the church, empowering teams, organizations, and societies to thrive. Whether leading congregations, organizing events, or building communities, pastors inspire collaboration and shared vision that reflects the order and love of God's kingdom.

GROWTH AREAS FOR PASTORS

Guarding Against Burnout

Burnout is a silent thief in pastoral ministry, stealing joy, strength, and clarity when left unchecked. As pastors, we pour ourselves out daily—praying, counselling, teaching, and leading—but without intentional replenishment, we risk becoming spiritually, emotionally, and physically drained. Even Jesus, fully God and fully man, modeled the importance of stepping away to rest and recharge: *"Come aside by yourselves to a deserted place and rest a while."* (Mark 6:31) Rest is not indulgence; it is obedience. It is the rhythm of grace that keeps us effective in our calling.

You might notice burnout creeping in when frustration arises at even the smallest interruptions, or when weariness weighs heavier than your love for the people you serve. Rest does not always require an expensive vacation or extended time away. For me, rest can mean retreating into God's presence for an hour, meditating in silence, or simply stepping away for a few days to recalibrate. Understand what rest looks like for you, and put systems in place to protect that time. Let rest become part of your ministry because a rested pastor is a thriving pastor.

Encouraging Interdependence

One of the greatest temptations in pastoral leadership is creating dependency. While our hearts long to nurture and protect, our goal must be to lead people to maturity in Christ—not to ourselves. A healthy flock does not lean solely on the shepherd but learns to seek God personally. As Hebrews 5:12 admonishes, *"By this time, you ought to be teachers..."* Pastors are entrusted with the responsibility to equip believers for growth, teaching them to hear from the Holy Spirit, study the Word, and walk in faith.

When someone is new in their faith, we often act as their primary connection to God, answering every question and walking closely with them. But as they grow, our role transitions to guiding them toward greater reliance on God Himself. I tell people, "Ask the Holy Spirit first, and if clarity doesn't come, I'll help you." This is not about abandoning them but preparing them to stand firm in Christ. The goal is raising people is not to create followers of the pastor but disciples of Christ who thrive spiritually, both individually and collectively.

Navigating Offence with Wisdom

A pastor's compassion makes them deeply invested in the lives of their flock. But that same compassion can also make them vulnerable to offence when their care is met with ingratitude or criticism. Proverbs 4:23 says, *"Keep your heart with all diligence, for out of it spring the issues of life."* Offence is a trap from the enemy, designed to shut down the flow of grace in your ministry.

There was a time when a minister of the gospel asked me, "On a scale of one to ten with ten as the highest, how much do you like your congregation?" My response was ten. Suffice it to say that the minister was surprised to hear my response. The question he asked surprised me, but it uncovered a deeper issue that many pastors harbour resentment towards their flock. Offence poisons the heart and clouds the ability to lead with love. To overcome it, pastors must keep their hearts guarded, remembering that their service is unto God. When you release offence and operate from a place of grace, you can minister freely, reflecting Christ's forgiveness and compassion.

Balancing Burdens and Boundaries

The pastoral call is deeply personal, often involving walking closely with people through their pain and struggles. While this connection is a blessing, it can also become a burden if not handled wisely. Pastors must remember that they are not the Saviour—only Jesus can carry the weight of the world. *"Casting all your care upon Him, for He cares for you."* (1 Peter 5:7). Establishing healthy boundaries is not a sign of indifference; it is a way to ensure the sustainability of your ministry and the preservation of your well-being.

How do you cast your burdens onto Jesus? By staying in constant fellowship with Him through your unique channel of grace. For me, that channel is meditation. As I go about my daily routines and duties, I meditate continuously, remaining intimately connected with God. This practice keeps me in tune with His voice, ensures I am drawing from His strength, and allows me to receive divine wisdom with ease. Your channel of grace might be prayer, faith in the Word, association with others, or worship. Whatever it is, identify it and nurture it.

When you remain close to the Shepherd, His grace becomes your strength, and His wisdom becomes your compass. This is the key to balancing the demands of empathy with reliance on God. By allowing Him to carry what you cannot, you can minister effectively without being consumed by the weight of others' struggles. Remember, you are a vessel, not the source. Let His grace flow through you, empowering you to care deeply while standing firmly in your own strength.

Embrace the Gift of Armour Bearers

As pastors, it is essential to recognize and embrace the ministry of armor bearers—those God has graced to care for you in love and honor. These individuals are more than helpers; they are divinely assigned partners who stand alongside you, sharing the weight of the calling and ensuring you remain strengthened and supported.

My wife and I have intentionally surrounded ourselves with such individuals—not because we are unable to fulfill the responsibilities of ministry but because we recognize the wisdom of allowing others to share the load. As Moses experienced with Aaron and Hur holding up his hands during the battle (Exodus 17:12), pastors need armour bearers who provide unwavering support. Their presence allows the work of ministry to continue without interruption, ensuring that the vision moves forward.

The posture of the heart is critical for anyone serving as an armour bearer. Their service must be rooted in love and carried out with honour, not out of obligation or self-interest. This role requires humility, integrity, and a genuine desire to see the pastor thrive in their calling. An armour bearer's effectiveness is in their actions and in the purity of their heart as they serve.

Allowing yourself to be ministered to by these burden bearers creates a rhythm of replenishment. While God renews your inner strength and provides revelation, armour bearers minister outwardly, enabling you to remain healthy, whole, and equipped for the journey ahead. Embracing their support is not a sign of weakness but of wisdom and trust in God's design for the body of Christ.

Fostering Continual Growth and Development

Pastors are called to be lifelong learners, continually growing in knowledge, wisdom, and grace. This growth is not only about acquiring knowledge but also about receiving fresh revelation from God. As 2 Timothy 2:15 exhorts, *"Be diligent to present yourself approved to God, a worker who does not need to be ashamed, rightly dividing the word of truth."* Time spent with God is not just preparation for ministry—it is nourishment for the soul. It is in His presence that pastors are renewed, equipped, and empowered to do more and handle more.

The Word of God is not only the foundation for your teaching but also a personal source of life and strength. When you spend time with God and receive His revelation, your capacity to lead, guide, and minister effectively increases. Revelation transforms your understanding and sharpens your ability to discern and act with wisdom. It positions you to carry greater responsibilities without being overwhelmed, as His grace flows abundantly through you.

Investing in your growth—whether through studying the Word, meditating on His promises, or seeking His guidance—ensures that your ministry remains impactful and relevant. Ministry flows from the overflow, so prioritize time with God. In Him, you will find the strength, wisdom, and revelation needed to fulfill your calling with grace and effectiveness.

Discernment in Helping Others

Pastors are natural helpers, but not every situation requires intervention, and not every individual is ready to receive help. *"Ask, and it will be given to you; seek, and you will find; knock, and it will be opened to you."* (Matthew 7:7). Discernment allows you to steward your time and energy wisely, ensuring that your efforts are directed where they will bear fruit.

Helping does not always mean doing everything yourself. Sometimes it means referring individuals to specialists or simply stepping back and trusting God to work in their lives. Discernment helps you distinguish between those who need your guidance and those who must learn to apply the wisdom already given.

Neglecting the Needs of Those They Serve

What we find in Ezekiel 34:1-10 is not an exciting thing to read.

"And the word of the Lord came to me, saying, "Son of man, prophesy against the shepherds of Israel, prophesy and say to them, 'Thus says the Lord God to the shepherds: 'Woe to the shepherds of Israel who feed themselves! Should not the shepherds feed the flocks? You eat the fat and clothe yourselves with the wool; you slaughter the fatlings, but you do not feed the flock. The weak you have not strengthened, nor have you healed those who were sick, nor bound up

the broken, nor brought back what was driven away, nor sought what was lost; but with force and cruelty you have ruled them. So, they were scattered because there was no shepherd; and they became food for all the beasts of the field when they were scattered. My sheep wandered through all the mountains, and on every high hill; yes, My flock was scattered over the whole face of the earth, and no one was seeking or searching for them." 'Therefore, you shepherds, hear the word of the Lord: "As I live," says the Lord God, "surely because My flock became a prey, and My flock became food for every beast of the field, because there was no shepherd, nor did My shepherds search for My flock, but the shepherds fed themselves and did not feed My flock"— therefore, O shepherds, hear the word of the Lord! Thus says the Lord God: "Behold, I am against the shepherds, and I will require My flock at their hand; I will cause them to cease feeding the sheep, and the shepherds shall feed themselves no more; for I will deliver My flock from their mouths, that they may no longer be food for them." (Ezekiel 34:1-10)

In this passage, God was scolding and correcting bad pastors. It is a sobering reminder of the consequences of pastoral neglect: *"Woe to the shepherds of Israel who feed themselves! Should not the shepherds feed the flock?"* Pastors are entrusted with God's people, and neglecting their needs is a breach of that trust.

A faithful pastor knows the state of their flock, follows up with care, and ensures no one is overlooked. Neglect can manifest as watered-down sermons, lack of follow-up, or fear-driven leadership. God calls pastors to shepherd His people with diligence, defending the flock and leading them into abundance.

Biblical Examples of Pastors

Jesus Christ

Jesus, the ultimate model of a pastor, provided compassionate care, guidance, and protection to His disciples and the multitudes. His example of sacrificial love and shepherding is the gold standard for all pastors. His life and ministry embody the principles of pastoral care, demonstrating the heart of a true shepherd.

In John 10:11-16, Jesus differentiates between a good shepherd and a hireling (a false shepherd). The good shepherd gives his life for the flock; he is sacrificial. In contrast, the hireling is only concerned with what they can receive and abandons the sheep when they are in danger. Jesus is the one and only good shepherd, and as pastors, we ought to follow His example. The pastor's job is to ensure that wolves do not scatter the sheep, but not much can be done for a sheep that chooses to follow wolves. Everyone has a decision to make.

"I am the good shepherd. The good shepherd gives His life for the sheep. But a hireling, he who is not the shepherd, one who does not own the sheep, sees the wolf coming and leaves the sheep and flees; and the wolf catches the sheep and scatters them. The hireling flees because he is a hireling and does not care about the sheep. I am the good shepherd; and I know My sheep and am known by My own. As the Father knows Me, even so I know the Father; and I lay down My life for the sheep. And other sheep I have which are not of this fold; them also I must bring, and they will hear My voice; and there will be one flock and one shepherd."

David

David exemplifies the pastoral heart through his psalms and leadership as king, caring for Israel with a shepherd's mindset. His compassion and dedication to his people reflect the essential qualities of a pastor. *"The Lord is my shepherd; I shall not want."* (Psalms 23:1) David's life as a shepherd and king provides valuable insights into the nature of pastoral leadership, balancing authority with compassion.

David's heart and actions as a shepherd, defending his flock from lions and bears, reflect the protective and caring nature of a pastor. His willingness to risk his life for his sheep showcases the essence of pastoral care.

"But David said to Saul, 'Your servant used to keep his father's sheep, and when a lion or a bear came and took a lamb out of the flock, I went out after it and struck it, and delivered the lamb from its mouth...'" (1 Samuel 17:34-35)

Paul

Though primarily an apostle, Paul's pastoral care for the churches he established is evident throughout his epistles. He provided guidance, correction, and encouragement, showing a deep commitment to the well-being of his congregations. *"[I] do not cease to give thanks for you, making mention of you in my prayers [.]"* (Ephesians 1:16) Paul's letters reveal his pastoral heart, addressing the spiritual and practical needs of the early church.

In *Acts 20:27-32*, Paul was speaking like a pastor. Paul was aware that so long as he was there, no attack from the enemy could succeed against his flock, but he also knew that after he left if those in charge were not on guard, an enemy could strike the flock.

"For I have not shunned to declare to you the whole counsel of God. Therefore take heed to yourselves and to all the flock, among which the Holy Spirit has made you overseers, to shepherd the church of God which He purchased with His own blood. For I know this, that after my departure savage wolves will come in among you, not sparing the flock. Also from among yourselves men will rise up, speaking perverse things, to draw away the disciples after themselves. Therefore watch, and remember that for three years I did not cease to warn everyone night and day with tears. So now, brethren, I commend you to God and to the word of His grace, which is able to build you up and give you an inheritance among all those who are sanctified."

Timothy

As a young pastor, Timothy received mentorship from Paul and demonstrated pastoral care and leadership in the early church. His dedication to serving and guiding his community sets a powerful example for pastoral ministry. *"Let no one despise your youth; instead, you should be an example to the believers in speech, in conduct, in love, in faith, in purity."* (1 Timothy 4:12) Timothy's life and ministry illustrate the importance of mentorship and the impact of pastoral care on a growing church.

6

The Teaching Office

INTRODUCTION TO THE TEACHING OFFICE

The teaching office, also known as the role of the teacher, is instrumental in the body of Christ and beyond. Serving as the immune system that identifies, preserves, and communicates truth to others, this office is vital in eliminating deception and ensuring that the truth is rightly divided. The significance of this office extends beyond the church to various sectors, including educational institutions, corporate training, healthcare, and any profession that involves sharing knowledge.

The Calling of a Teacher

Many do not realize how important a teacher is to society, the church, and every group. For example, John 8:32 says, *"You shall know the truth, and the truth shall set you free."* A teacher is an agent of deliverance, transformation, and restoration, helping people get to where they are supposed to be and keeping them there.

A teacher's role provides stability. When someone builds their life on the truth, they are more likely to be stable in every area of life. They avoid unnecessary battles, live in freedom, and experience liberty. This role is so vital that the core office Jesus Christ identified with was "Rabbi," meaning teacher.

Strangely, the teaching office is often the most overlooked. In the body of Christ, it is rare to see someone identify as a teacher in their title. It is common to hear titles like Apostle, Prophet, Evangelist, or Pastor, but rarely Teacher. It almost feels out of place. This is significant because there is an assault on truth. Now, more than ever, we need teachers to rise, teach with clarity and love, and take on the responsibility of quality assurance, acting as the immune system of society.

In society, the media operates as a form of the teaching office. Journalists, for example, are often called the Fourth Estate because they hold other levels of government accountable. In a proper society, journalists and media are given the freedom to challenge, enforce, and clarify the truth without interference from the government. Societies where media can function freely, ethically, and properly often experience prosperity.

CHARACTERISTICS OF A TEACHER

Passion For Knowledge and Understanding

Teachers have an innate desire to learn and understand. They are constantly seeking new knowledge, not just for its own sake but to deepen their comprehension and insight. This thirst goes far beyond casual interest; it is a driving force in their lives, pushing them to read, study, and explore various subjects in-depth. It's not enough for teachers to know something;

they deeply desire to understand it fully. They are adept at making connections between different pieces of information and enjoy unravelling the intricacies of a topic to achieve a deep, coherent comprehension. They aim to demystify complex ideas and present them in a way others can easily understand.

Teachers possess a natural thirst for knowledge. However, if not reined in, this attraction to information can sometimes lead them to unprofitable pursuits, such as gossip. Teachers must discern between beneficial knowledge and that which should be avoided, always striving to seek the truth that edifies, builds up the body of Christ, and enhances their professional fields

Teachers also have a natural ability to understand anything they set their minds to. They act like a flashlight that can illuminate dark areas, making complex things clear and comprehensible. For example, when King Solomon looked at the ants in Proverbs 6:6-11 and understood them, it was the teaching grace in action. The Book of Proverbs, filled with practical wisdom, is a testament to the deep understanding that comes with the teaching gift.

Commitment to Truth

Central to the teaching office is a profound commitment to truth. Teachers uphold truth as a foundational value, ensuring that their instruction is reliable, ethically sound, and grounded in accurate information. This passion for truth underpins their desire to teach others, ensuring their teachings are trustworthy and grounded in scripture and verified information. They are detail-oriented and often require more than summaries to ensure clarity and accuracy. Teachers act as the immune system of the Body of Christ, combating false teachings and misunderstandings, much like white blood cells fight off diseases. By pursuing and defending truth, teachers fulfill a vital calling to preserve both spiritual and intellectual health. This office is crucial within the church, where doctrinal integrity is essential, and in fields like journalism, academia, and law, where the accuracy of information is paramount.

Detail-Oriented

Teachers are meticulous and pay close attention to details. They ensure that every aspect of their teaching is accurate, comprehensive, and aligned with biblical truth or established knowledge. This detailed approach means they may explain things in much greater depth than others, breaking down complex ideas into digestible parts. Their methodical nature helps learners grasp nuanced concepts more clearly, leaving little room for confusion or doubt. This attribute is crucial in fields such as law, medicine, and academia, where precision is paramount.

Extended Explanations

Teachers possess a remarkable ability to engage in extended discussions, often speaking at length with depth and clarity. This tendency stems from their wealth of information and insight, which they are eager to share. They thrive on exploring topics from various angles, dissecting ideas with meticulous care, and ensuring every detail is understood.

This trait is one of your greatest strengths. In spaces like workshops, seminars, and lectures, your ability to elaborate and engage creates a rich and immersive learning environment. Your listeners depend on your thoroughness; they expect you to connect the dots, clarify ambiguities, and expand on ideas that might otherwise remain vague.

A Love For Helping Others Understand

Teachers are naturally inclined to share their knowledge with others. They derive joy from helping others achieve understanding. Their ability to simplify and present complex ideas in relatable terms makes them compelling communicators. They use various methods, such as analogies, stories, and visual aids, to ensure their listeners can grasp and apply the teachings to their lives.

Teachers have the unique ability to make complex theological concepts accessible to everyone. Using clear and straightforward language, they break down intricate ideas into manageable parts. This ensures that all believers, regardless of their level of understanding, can grasp and apply biblical principles. Their teaching enables the church to grow in knowledge and spiritual maturity. This skill is also vital in settings like universities, training programs, and development workshops where complex ideas must be communicated effectively.

Immune System of the Church

Just as the immune system protects the body from diseases, teachers safeguard the church from false doctrines and teachings. They uphold sound doctrine and biblical truth, ensuring the church remains spiritually healthy and grounded. Teachers are vigilant in identifying and correcting errors, providing a shield against misleading interpretations of scripture. By preserving the integrity of biblical doctrine, teachers help maintain the church's faithfulness to Christ. This role also extends to educational institutions and other professions that require safeguarding truth and accuracy.

Revivals and movements are vulnerable to strange doctrines and heresies without sound teaching. Teachers ground these movements in biblical truth, protecting them from doctrinal errors. By upholding sound teaching, they help maintain order and truth within the church, preventing deviances that could lead believers astray. This protective role is equally vital in academia, corporate settings, and other areas where maintaining the integrity of information is crucial.

GROWTH AREAS FOR TEACHERS

Avoid Discouragement

The teaching office is pivotal in the body of Christ, yet you may often feel it's underappreciated and misunderstood. Unlike the more visible roles of apostles and prophets, your contributions might sometimes go unnoticed, leaving you questioning your impact or even feeling inadequate.

But the truth is that your calling is irreplaceable. You are the one who nurtures spiritual growth, equips believers with knowledge, and helps others deepen their understanding of God's Word. Without you, the foundation of the church would lack clarity and direction. When you recognize that every office is vital to the church's health, you can stand firm in your purpose. Your worth isn't determined by visibility but by the lives you transform through your teaching. The same principle applies in educational or professional environments. While other roles might seem more celebrated, your ability to illuminate and equip others is what ensures progress and lasting impact.

Communicating For Their Pleasure

For many teachers, teaching is a source of profound joy and fulfillment. Their passion for breaking down complex ideas and bringing clarity often drives them to go above and beyond in their explanations. However, this enthusiasm can sometimes lead to over-explaining, even when their audience has already grasped the material.

While your desire to share knowledge is admirable, it is vital for you to strike a balance between your passion for teaching and the needs of your audience. Practicing brevity and being sensitive to the cues of the audience are marks of a skilled teacher. This approach not only honors the time of the learners but also ensures that the message is impactful and digestible, leaving no room for overwhelm or fatigue.

Much like a wise chef who knows to stop serving food when the diners are satisfied, you must learn to stop teaching when the audience has received what they need—not when you have run out of things to say. This requires the discipline of self-control, a skill that must be deliberately cultivated through intentional practice.

Frustration When They Don't Understand Things

Teachers may experience frustration when confronted with concepts or issues that elude their understanding, feeling as though their ability to teach is compromised. In such moments, it is crucial for them to remember that true understanding comes from God. There are instances when God may intentionally withhold understanding to cultivate humility and dependence on Him. Embracing this reality allows teachers to navigate feelings of helplessness and confusion with grace, fostering a spirit of inquiry and reliance on divine guidance. Ensure that you do not allow a lack of understanding to negatively impact your emotions. Maintain your joy regardless of whether you understand a concept or not. Learn to draw understanding from others who have the understanding and humbly learn from them. In other instances, you might have to read over a concept a few times to understand.

Unnecessary Information Gathering

In the quest for knowledge, teachers must be discerning about the information they pursue. The abundance of resources available today can lead to the temptation of gathering excessive information, some of which may be irrelevant or misleading. Teachers should establish boundaries in their research, focusing on credible sources that align with sound doctrine. By prioritizing purposeful and directed learning, teachers can ensure that their knowledge is both beneficial and applicable, enhancing their teaching effectiveness without becoming bogged down by unnecessary details.

Discerning When to Teach Knowledge or Act on It

A common challenge for teachers is the distinction between possessing theoretical knowledge and having the practical skills to implement that knowledge. It is vital for teachers to recognize that teaching and executing a task are separate endeavors. This understanding encourages them to approach their role with wisdom and discernment, ensuring they not only convey information but also model the application of that knowledge in real-world contexts. By doing so, they can inspire their students to translate learning into action.

Engage in Lifelong Learning

As a teacher, you are called to be a lifelong learner, constantly seeking to grow in knowledge and understanding. This commitment to ongoing personal and professional development ensures that your teaching remains effective, impactful, and relevant. The Bible reminds us in 2 Timothy 2:15, *"Be diligent to present yourself approved to God, a worker who does not need to be ashamed, rightly dividing the word of truth."* This diligence applies not only to spiritual matters but also to the continual pursuit of excellence in every area of teaching.

Lifelong learning empowers you to address contemporary issues with wisdom and integrate fresh insights into your teachings, ensuring that those under your care receive guidance that is both timely and transformative. Think of knowledge as a flowing river—when the water moves freely, it remains fresh and healthy, fit for consumption. However, when the flow stops, the river becomes stagnant and unfit to serve its purpose.

In the same way, a teacher who neglects lifelong learning risks becoming stagnant, unable to meet the evolving needs of their students or congregation. Let the commitment to growth and discovery be the hallmark of your teaching ministry, keeping your knowledge vibrant and your impact lasting.

Develop Clear Communication Skills

As a teacher, your ability to convey complex ideas in simple, accessible, and relatable terms is essential to your calling. The truth you carry must not only be understood but also embraced by those you teach, and this requires intentionality in how you communicate. Utilizing analogies, stories, and visual aids can significantly enhance understanding and retention among learners.

Over the years, I've had to invest in refining this skill—whether through effective communication courses or by reading books dedicated to mastering it. I've come to understand that knowing the truth is one thing but being able to deliver it effectively to different demographics, races, and groups is another entirely.

Some teachers may find that verbal communication comes naturally, while others may excel in written forms of expression. Both are valuable, and neither should be neglected. Every opportunity to sharpen your communication skills should be embraced wholeheartedly. Whether through practice, feedback, or intentional study, remember that your effectiveness as a teacher hinges on your ability to clearly and powerfully convey the message entrusted to you.

Foster Critical Thinking

Encouraging critical thinking is essential for developing independent learners. Teachers should challenge students with thought-provoking questions and facilitate discussions that encourage deeper exploration of the subject matter. By promoting an environment where questioning and exploration are welcomed, teachers can help students analyze assumptions and develop their own understanding. This approach fosters a culture of inquiry that is far more effective than merely providing all the answers. As mentioned earlier, teachers can tend to be satisfied by the process of communicating information to others. While this is true, there must be a balance between allowing the learning to find the information themselves under the careful guidance of a teacher. This balanced approach will help the teacher to raise a true interdependent learner as opposed to a dependent learner.

Build Relationships

Building strong relationships with students or congregants is vital for creating a supportive and effective learning environment. Teachers should strive to understand the unique needs, challenges, and aspirations of their learners. Establishing rapport fosters trust and engagement, making it easier for students to absorb and apply the teachings. This relational aspect is crucial across all teaching contexts, from Sunday school to university classrooms and corporate training sessions.

BIBLICAL EXAMPLES OF TEACHERS

Jesus Christ

Jesus Christ, the cornerstone of our faith, was the epitome of a teacher. Throughout His ministry, He was often addressed as 'Rabbi,' a testament to His revered status as a teacher. His teachings were not just mere words but life-transforming truths that have shaped the course of history. In John 1:38, when His disciples addressed Him as "Rabbi," it was a recognition of His profound teaching authority. Jesus' parables and sermons, like the Sermon on the Mount, were masterclasses in conveying divine wisdom in relatable terms. His teachings continue to be the bedrock of Christian doctrine, guiding believers in their walk with God.

Paul the Apostle

Paul, though primarily an apostle, was also a distinguished teacher. His epistles are a treasure trove of doctrinal insights and practical guidance, reflecting his dedication to educating the early church. In Romans, Paul meticulously explains the gospel, tackling complex topics like justification by faith and the role of the law. His teachings on spiritual gifts, love, and resurrection in 1 Corinthians demonstrate his deep understanding and ability to communicate theological truths effectively. Paul's writings remain a guiding light for believers, showcasing the enduring impact of the teaching office.

Solomon

Solomon, known for his unparalleled wisdom, exemplified the teaching grace through his writings in Proverbs and Ecclesiastes. His ability to distill profound truths into simple, everyday wisdom is a hallmark of the teaching gift. Proverbs, a collection of wise sayings, provides timeless guidance on practical living, relationships, and spirituality. Solomon's teachings emphasize the importance of wisdom and understanding, offering insights that have been cherished across generations.

Apollos

Apollos, a man of great learning and fervour, was a powerful teacher in the early church. Initially acquainted only with the baptism of John, his teaching prowess was further honed by Priscilla and Aquila, who explained the way of God more accurately to him. Apollos' eloquence and fervour in teaching made him a formidable figure, as he vigorously refuted the Jews in public debate, proving from the Scriptures that Jesus was the Messiah (Acts 18:24-28).

Ezra

Ezra, a scribe skilled in the Law of Moses, was dedicated to studying, practicing, and teaching God's statutes. His role as a teacher was crucial in the spiritual reformation of the Jewish people after their return from exile. Ezra's commitment to teaching God's laws helped restore religious and social order, as he read the Law to the people and explained its meaning, ensuring they understood and applied it to their lives (Ezra 7:6, 10).

Timothy

Timothy, though primarily known as a pastor and protégé of Paul, was entrusted with significant teaching responsibilities. Paul encouraged him to be diligent in teaching, rightly dividing the word of truth and instructing others in sound doctrine. Timothy's role was vital in the early church, particularly in countering false teachings and maintaining the integrity of the gospel message. His example underscores the importance of mentorship and the transmission of sound teaching to future generations.

7

The Interdependence of the Five-Fold Offices

While each role is distinct in its function, none can operate in isolation. Each office relies on others to fulfill the shared mission of edifying the body and advancing God's ultimate purpose. By embracing their unique callings and working in harmony, the Five-Fold Offices create a synergy that ensures the body remains balanced, mature, and fully equipped for every good work.

MUTUAL DEPENDENCE

The Five-Fold Ministry functions best when there is interdependence rather than independence. Each office contributes unique strengths and relies on the others to fulfill a holistic mission. Apostles set the vision, prophets bring divine insight, evangelists expand the mission, pastors nurture and care for the people, and teachers ground everyone in truth. Together, they form a seamless collaboration that benefits the body of Christ and extends into various spheres of influence.

ILLUSTRATIONS OF THE INTERPLAY BETWEEN OFFICES

The Five-Fold Offices bring unique strengths and perspectives. Each office plays a distinct yet interconnected role in God's plan, ensuring the spiritual health, growth, and balance of the body of Christ.

- **The Apostle** provides visionary leadership, initiating and strategizing to advance the mission.

- **The Prophet** offers foresight and confirmation, revealing divine truth and direction.

- **The Evangelist** inspires and gathers, engaging in passionate outreach to bring others into the fold.

- **The Pastor** nurtures and protects, fostering a sense of care and belonging within the community.

- **The Teacher** ensures understanding, grounding people in knowledge and guiding them with clarity.

These roles complement one another, forming a cohesive framework for ministry. Here are several ways to understand the contributions of each office:

Functional Perspectives of the Offices

Leadership Dynamics: The apostle governs. The prophet guides. The evangelist gathers. The pastor guards. The teacher grounds and equips.

Types of Vision: The apostle has long sight or a broad strategic view. The prophet has foresight, perceiving what lies ahead. The evangelist has hindsight, leveraging their passion to reach more people. The pastor has oversight, ensuring care for the community. The teacher has insight, explaining and maintaining clarity.

Analogies for the Offices: The apostle is a visionary strategist who maps out the future. The prophet is a spiritual advisor, providing divine perspective. The evangelist is a persuasive communicator, igniting enthusiasm for the mission. The pastor is a human resources manager, fostering relationships and well-being. The teacher is a logical thinker or implementer, ensuring understanding and application.

In the Human Body: The apostle is the brain, coordinating vision and action. The prophet represents the five senses, perceiving what others may miss. The evangelist is the muscles, driving movement and action. The pastor is the skeletal system, providing structure and support. The teacher is the immune system, preserving integrity and correcting errors.

Impact of Missing Offices

The absence of any office creates imbalance and hinders the effectiveness of the body of Christ:

Without apostolic leadership, the foundation weakens. Without prophetic insight, deception creeps in. Without evangelistic fervor, the message remains hidden. Without pastoral care, communities fall into disorder. Without teaching, misunderstandings spread.

This same principle applies to secular organizations. A well-functioning organization mirrors the Five-Fold Offices to achieve its goals:

- **Apostle:** Business Development, Strategy, Talent and Learning Development

- **Prophet:** Health and Safety, Innovation, Research and Development

- **Evangelist:** Sales, Marketing, Brand Management

- **Pastor:** Human Resources, Operations

- **Teacher:** Quality Assurance, Business Analytics, Data Science

Each role—apostle, evangelist, teacher, pastor, and prophet—ensures each community's health and balance, echoing the need for a comprehensive understanding and experience of the vision or mission at stake.

The Five-Fold Offices As Beverages

What is Your Drink?

5 FOLD OFFICES
Drink Types

VERSATILE

STRONG
&SELF-DRIVEN

GIFTED TO
START NEW
THINGS

LEADERSHIP ABILITY

FOCUSED &
STRAIGHTFORWARD

GETS THE JOB DONE

The Apostle: Dark Roast

The Apostle

The Prophet

The Evangelist

5 FOLD OFFICES
Drink Types

LOVED BY EVERYONE

COMFORTING & WARM

GOOD AT GIVING ADVICE

SUPPORTIVE & PROTECTIVE

BRINGS PEOPLE TOGETHER

The Pastor: Hot Chocolate

The Pastor

The Teacher

Ultimately, understanding and embracing these diverse contributions enrich our spiritual journey, fostering a balanced and healthy body of believers united in purpose and mission.

OVERCOMING CHALLENGES IN SYNERGY

Achieving synergy among diverse roles within the body of Christ is not without its challenges. Differing perspectives, each shaped by a unique vocational calling, can often lead to misunderstanding or even tension. As a leader, it is your responsibility to proactively foster an environment where mutual respect and honest communication are the foundation. Instead of viewing differences as obstacles, recognize them as opportunities for growth. By encouraging open dialogue and practicing patient listening, you create a culture where collaboration thrives. This requires careful balance—ensuring that no single role dominates while no other is marginalized.

Cultural and personal differences among leaders and team members further add complexity to the pursuit of synergy. Bridging these gaps requires intentional effort, including inclusivity, ongoing training, and team-building exercises. Leaders set the tone by demonstrating empathy, cultural sensitivity, and a genuine willingness to learn from others. By remaining adaptable and ready to adjust strategies as circumstances change, you can guide your team without losing sight of the overarching mission.

Other two significant hindrances to achieving synergy are **Shame** and **Jealousy**.

Dealing with Shame

Shame, whether directed at ourselves or others, can hinder the unity and effectiveness of the Five-Fold Offices. If not addressed, it distorts our understanding of the value God has placed in each office and prevents us from appreciating the diversity within the body of Christ. To overcome shame, we must approach this issue with grace, wisdom, and humility.

First, it is crucial to resist the urge to shame others. No office is lesser or greater than another in God's design. It may be tempting to think the grass is greener on the other side or to criticize a role that doesn't resemble ours. However, each office has a unique purpose and grace that contributes to the whole body. Looking down on others diminishes the harmony God intended. Honour for one another is the foundation of unity, and when we dishonour any part of the body, we dishonour the entire body.

Do not let someone else's mistakes or weaknesses distort your view of their calling. For example, being hurt by an apostle does not mean all apostles are heartless. Similarly, encountering a loud evangelist who struggles with self-control does not mean all evangelists lack discipline. Treat each person as an individual rather than judging entire offices based on a single experience.

In the same vein, we must guard against shaming ourselves. Sometimes, we believe that another office is "better" or "more important" than ours, leading to unnecessary comparisons and a diminished sense of purpose. This is a lie that robs us of the joy and glory of our calling. God placed each of us in our specific roles intentionally, knowing what we carry and where we are most effective. Embrace your office with confidence, knowing that it is a vital part of God's plan.

Personal insecurities can further complicate matters, but they can be addressed and overcome. Like an outfit, it is the person wearing it who determines whether it looks glorious or not. This means our own insecurities can hinder the full expression of our office. We must work with the Holy Spirit to deal with these insecurities.

It is also important to recognize that every office has both glory and the potential for shame. The key lies in how we choose to partner with the Holy Spirit. When we walk in humility and wisdom, we can bring out the best in our offices while addressing and suppressing the weaknesses. No one is perfect, but with God's guidance, we can refine our gifts and steward our roles in ways that glorify Him. This process requires intentionality and a heart submitted to God's will.

While shame can be transferable, glory can be as well. Instead of focusing on the negative, seek out role models who exemplify the beauty and power of their offices. Observe apostles who lead with grace and wisdom, evangelists who reach others with love and compassion, or teachers who inspire and encourage through their insight. Let these examples remind you of the potential and honour in every role. Celebrate the positive expressions of each office, and allow them to shape your understanding.

Covet Gifts, Not Offices

Offices in the Body of Christ carry immense responsibility. They are not positions to be coveted for recognition or status but roles requiring unwavering commitment to serve God and His people faithfully. If you desire to step into an office, you must be willing to embrace its responsibilities, challenges, and sacrifices. These roles are not about personal glory; they are about serving God and His people faithfully.

But let me show you a better way: coveting gifts, not offices. A gift, once given by God, becomes yours to steward for His glory. Unlike offices, which come with structured roles and expectations, gifts empower you to function effectively in whichever office God has placed you. Instead of longing for someone else's office, seek the gifts that will enhance your effectiveness within your unique calling.

Jealousy often arises when we laser focus on roles others are playing, coveting their offices rather than appreciating the gifts God has given them to operate seamlessly in that role. This mindset can hinder growth and breed discontentment. Instead, focus on developing the gifts God has already placed within you while seeking new ones that will expand your capacity. For example, if you are called to the pastoral office, you can still operate in the gifts associated with the apostolic, evangelistic, prophetic, and teaching roles. These gifts are not confined to specific offices but can be accessed and utilized to support your primary calling.

Consider the example of Christ. While His ministry reflected a pastoral heart, He also demonstrated the fullness of spiritual gifts. He taught with authority, prophesied with accuracy, evangelized with passion, and built the Kingdom with apostolic strategy. Christ was not confined to a single role—He operated in every gift necessary to fulfill His purpose. He sets the standard for us to follow, showing that it's not about striving for a title but about embracing the gifts that allow us to serve effectively.

Jealousy has no place in the Body of Christ. Instead of envying someone else's office, celebrate the diversity of callings and seek the spiritual gifts that will help you thrive in your unique purpose. When you covet gifts, not offices, you position yourself to operate in freedom, effectiveness, and alignment with God's plan.

Pathways to Achieving Synergy

Synergy within the Five-Fold Offices begins with understanding that we are designed to work together as one body. Each office carries unique responsibilities and graces, but none is complete without the others. To foster this interdependence, it is crucial to equip leaders and teams with the knowledge and skills to truly appreciate the value of every office. Workshops, conferences, and intentional teaching sessions can illuminate how these roles are meant to connect and complement each other. As relationships are nurtured—through mentorship, informal gatherings, and open forums—trust and camaraderie naturally take root, making collaboration between offices fruitful.

A clear vision and mission are essential to unifying the Five-Fold Offices. When every activity is aligned with the ultimate purpose of the team or organization, it provides a solid framework for unity. As leaders, we must continually affirm this shared mission, celebrate the contributions of each office, and ensure accountability processes reflect a commitment to the collective good. It is in this environment of mutual respect and honour that the offices can truly thrive.

Practical steps, such as joint projects, events, and outreach initiatives, further strengthen these bonds. When apostles, prophets, evangelists, pastors, and teachers come together to serve side by side, the impact is multiplied, and a deeper appreciation for one another's roles begins to emerge. These shared experiences break down barriers and foster understanding, reminding everyone of the beauty of diversity within unity.

As leaders, we must model the collaboration we seek to inspire. By intentionally honoring the strengths and contributions of every office, we set the tone for others to follow. When unity is prioritized, when trust is cultivated, and when the collective mission is kept at the forefront, the Five-Fold Offices can function as one cohesive body. This is how we fulfill the divine mandate entrusted to us—by operating together, as God intended, to build His Kingdom and bring glory to His name.

Epilogue

As we conclude our exploration of the Five-Fold Offices, it is essential to reflect on the journey we've taken together in uncovering the unique and vital roles that apostles, prophets, evangelists, pastors, and teachers play in the Body of Christ and beyond. This journey is an intellectual exercise and a heartfelt endeavour to understand God's divine design for humanity and our collective and individual impact on the world.

IDENTITY IS A DELICATE MATTER

Understanding our role within the Five-Fold Ministry touches on the sensitive terrain of identity. We are not talking about mere titles or positions, but about embracing the purpose for which God created us. Perhaps you resonated with the apostle's pioneering spirit—an inner drive to establish new ministries, initiatives, or solutions that bring light to dark places. Maybe you felt the prophetic call, sensing God's voice and knowing He has called you to reveal His will in ways that guide individuals, organizations, and entire communities toward His truth. You may recognize yourself in the evangelist's passion to reach the lost, to share the good news of Christ in schools, neighbourhoods, and boardrooms, transforming societies through the gospel's power. If compassion and guidance define your heart, then you may naturally lean into the pastoral role, providing care and counsel in the church, on the mission field, or even in the counselling center. Or perhaps you find yourself most at home in the teacher's role, imparting wisdom, ensuring sound doctrine, and helping others navigate life's complexities with clear understanding.

Whichever calling resonates with you, consider where God has been leading you. Reflect on the ways He has stirred your heart. Are you already sensing the apostolic fire that compels you to build, or the prophetic insight that clarifies truth in uncertain times? Do you carry the evangelist's burden for those who have never heard the message of hope, or the pastor's compassionate pull to shepherd souls? You might love unveiling new truths, guiding people into deeper understanding as a teacher. These are not empty designations; they are God's way of equipping you for a unique mission. Embrace your calling fully, remembering that God has entrusted you with these gifts to serve others and reveal His heart to the world. If shame or uncertainty haunts you, bring it before God. Your role is neither an accident nor a mistake—it is intentional, purposeful, and precious in His sight.

Leave Others' Offices to God

As you affirm your own calling, resist the temptation to dictate how others should walk out theirs. Each person's journey with Christ is deeply personal and sacred. Leave their calling between them and God. Focus on living out your calling with authenticity, humility, and grace, trusting that the diversity of gifts is part of God's design rather than a point of contention.

A CALL TO ACTION

Let this book serve as both a guide and a challenge. Let it encourage you to assess your strengths, seek mentorship, and lean into the relationships and structures that support unified ministry. Bring your unique calling—be it apostolic, prophetic, evangelistic, pastoral, or teaching—into conversations, planning sessions, and daily interactions. Advocate for a culture where each office is respected and valued.

The future of the church and society depends on willingness of believers to heed this call. It rests on our determination to embrace our offices, honour one another's roles, and step into the world as agents of God's kingdom. Imagine a world where believers confidently walk in their unique offices, forging ministries that are strong, compassionate, and impactful. A world where every sphere of influence is touched by the light of Christ, every relationship enriched by His love, and every endeavour guided by divine wisdom.

Let us leave behind a legacy of a Church fully alive—one that reflects the fullness of Jesus through the Five-Fold Offices. As one body, we can shape history, transform lives, and advance God's kingdom. May we move forward with courage, unity, and unwavering faith, fulfilling our callings one community, one life, and one soul at a time.

Contact The Author

I know without a doubt that this book has been a blessing to you. I am looking forward to hearing your testimony.

You can stay connected with me through the following platforms:

Instagram: e.adewusi | **Youtube:** Emmanuel Adewusi
Website: emmanueladewusi.org

SUPPORT THE AUTHOR

Review the Book

A Sinner's Prayer

Dear Heavenly Father,

I come to You in the Name of Jesus Christ.

You said in Your Word, "Whosoever shall call upon the name of the Lord shall be saved." (Romans 10:13) I am calling on Your Name, so I know You have saved me now.

You also said that "if you confess with your mouth the Lord Jesus and believe in your heart that God has raised Him from the dead, you will be saved. For with the heart one believes unto righteousness, and with the mouth, confession is made unto salvation." (Romans 10:9-10) I believe in my heart Jesus Christ is the Son of God. I believe that He was raised from the dead for my justification, and I confess Him now as my Lord and Savior.

Thank you, Lord, because now, I am saved!

Thank You, Lord, because I know you have heard my prayer. Thank You, Lord, because I am now born again.

Signed _____

Date _____

About The Author

Apostle Emmanuel Adewusi is the Founding and Lead Pastor of Cornerstone Christian Church of God.

Called into ministry with the mandate to "bring restoration and transformation to all by teaching, preaching, and demonstrating the Gospel of Jesus Christ," he is passionate about seeing lives restored and transformed as God intended from the beginning of creation. He has a zeal for the full counsel of the Word of God, fellowship with the Holy Spirit, and being under spiritual authority.

He authored the books *"Now That You Are Born Again, What Next?", "The Blessings of Being Under Spiritual Authority," "A Disciplined Life," "The Enlightened Believer," "The Skilled Sower,"* and other impactful titles. He has also released an album titled *"Divine Encounter"* and many more on the way.

Emmanuel Adewusi is joyfully married to his wife, Ibukun Adewusi, and together, they are building a thriving Christ-centered family.

www.ingramcontent.com/pod-product-compliance
Lightning Source LLC
Chambersburg PA
CBHW050220270326
41914CB00003BA/505